The Joy of Knowing How to Learn

Language Skills
Series 2: Vocabulary
Level A, Grades 1-3

Joyce McPeake Robinson

2019

Pangrove Press

Available from Amazon.com and other retail outlets

The Joy of Knowing How to Learn

Language Skills: Vocabulary

Copyright © 2019

by

Joyce McPeake Robinson

Pangrove Press

All rights reserved worldwide. No part of this publication may be reproduced or transmitted in any form or by any means, electronic or mechanical, including photocopying, recording, scanning, photographing, or by any information storage and retrieval system.

Printed in the United States of America

About the Author: Dr. Joyce McPeake Robinson, an independent educational consultant, has a wealth of experience as teacher and school administrator. A graduate of Tufts University, she holds her master's and doctoral degrees from Boston University. Her major research interests include English language skills acquisition, literature analysis and curriculum development. An active member of the academic community, she has served on numerous boards of educational organizations and has received worldwide recognition for her achievements.

Pangrove Press

Table of Contents

INTRODUCTION 7

TO STUDENTS: 11

1. 100 STUDY SHEETS DIRECTIONS 12

   100 STUDY SHEETS 13

2. TESTS DIRECTIONS 214

   WORD GROUP 1 TEST: Words 1-10 216

   WORD GROUP 2 TEST: Words 11-20 218

   WORD GROUP 3 TEST: Words 21-30 220

   WORD GROUP 4 TEST: Words 31-40 222

   WORD GROUP 5 TEST: Words 41-50 224

   WORD GROUP 6 TEST: Words 51-60 226

   WORD GROUP 7 TEST: Words 61-70 228

   WORD GROUP 8 TEST: Words 71-80 230

   WORD GROUP 9 TEST: Words 81-90 232

   WORD GROUP 10 TEST: Words 91-100 234

3. TESTS ANSWER KEYS DIRECTIONS 236

   WORD GROUP 1 TEST ANSWER KEYS: Words 1-10 238

   WORD GROUP 2 TEST ANSWER KEYS: Words 11-20 240

   WORD GROUP 3 TEST ANSWER KEYS: Words 21-30 242

   WORD GROUP 4 TEST ANSWER KEYS: Words 31-40 244

   WORD GROUP 5 TEST ANSWER KEYS: Words 41-50 246

WORD GROUP 6 TEST ANSWER KEYS: Words 51-60 248

WORD GROUP 7 TEST ANSWER KEYS: Words 61-70 250

WORD GROUP 8 TEST ANSWER KEYS: Words 71-80 252

WORD GROUP 9 TEST ANSWER KEYS: Words 81-90 254

WORD GROUP 10 TEST ANSWER KEYS: Words 91-100 256

4. CHECKLISTS OF LEARNED WORDS DIRECTIONS 259

Word Groups 1 and 2 260

Word Groups 3 and 4 261

Word Groups 5 and 6 262

Word Groups 7 and 8 263

Word Groups 9 and 10 264

CONGRATULATIONS! 265

LIST OF STUDY WORDS 266

INTRODUCTION

The joy of learning comes from knowing exactly how to acquire the important basic language skills, the foundation for future success in academic and lifelong study. Without a command of communication tools, early learners especially cannot reach their full potential in reading, writing, speaking and listening.

Unfortunately, many learners move ahead to higher academic expectations, even if they have inadequate preparation. A hit or miss approach to learning predictably follows and increases the risk of poor performance and other negative consequences, including emotional issues and dropping out of school.

Building on the sound learning principles of *The Joy of Knowing How to Learn, Language Skills Series 1: Spelling,* this vocabulary workbook, second in the series, focuses on learning a study process and mastering 100 words commonly used among students in Grades 1-3.

The mastery of spelling skills involves using neural pathways that help all other language areas. Interestingly, recent neurolinguistic studies show improved brain activity patterns for learning all basic language skills after first gaining a sound basis in written spelling proficiency.

Correctly writing out words activates a stunning interaction among the visual, auditory, kinesthetic and tactile sensory receivers. The brain's input and output neural systems work to affect each other reciprocally. Brain circuitry studies also found that after becoming proficient in spelling words, dyslexic children had brain patterns that moved from abnormal to positive functioning. A readiness develops then for succeeding in other areas of language skills, such as word mastery.

Vocabulary is central to developing reading, writing, speaking and listening skills. Well documented in the educational research literature is that a meager knowledge of words leads to poor communication, as well as obstacles to further academic learning. The more words learned, the better students will be able to read, write, speak, listen and take full advantage of the rewards of language fluency.

Eventually, learners will internalize their own way to use this workbook's strategies, according to their individual learning styles and needs. As with other psychomotor skills, like bicycle riding or piano playing, learning words starts out with conscious actions that later become individualized, automatic strategies for building a firm foundation, on which to develop to higher learning levels. Likewise, learners who have mastered basic language skills no longer have to think about what words mean or how to write them. They can then follow wherever their ideas take them in reading and writing.

Students who have successfully used the proven learning program in this workbook series represent a wide range of learners, of varying ages, grades and backgrounds. Teachers and parents have documented significant improvement for those who benefit from direct language skills instruction, notably special needs students and English language learners.

Adaptations of this workbook can be helpful for accommodating individual learning needs. Typical adjustments include modifying the amount of study time and helping with reviewing directions, keeping in mind varying early learners' skill levels. As with all educational materials, decisions about individualizing instruction depend on a variety of factors, such as available assessments and observations.

You can also guide and involve learners in finding creative ways to continue expanding vocabulary opportunities, with the goal of steady practice of using words in meaningful writing experiences. They can build upon the workbook's examples of definitions and word usage by finding other meanings to add to their understanding of the mastered 100 words.

Additionally, effective ways to reinforce word knowledge includes writing daily journal entries, letters, shopping lists, labels, stories, poems, and personal dictionaries. Always keep in mind the interests and skill levels of learners.

This workbook series then can be viewed as a gift that keeps on giving. Knowing how to learn basic language skills to automaticity allows students to reach higher levels of communication skills with ease. Mastering reading, writing, speaking and listening then provides the opportunity for not only future academic success, but also for a lifetime of joyful independent learning.

TO STUDENTS: 🙂

Get set to put smiles on your face, as you learn a new way to master 100 helpful words!

You also will have a 10-step way for learning any other words you want to know.

Follow easy directions that come before each of the four parts of the workbook.

1. **Study Sheets - Directions:** page 13

2. **Tests - Directions:** page 214

3. **Tests Answer Keys - Directions:** page 236

4. **Checklists for Learned Words - Directions:** page 259

Now, turn the page to begin a lifetime of learning words!

1. 100 STUDY SHEETS

DIRECTIONS

HOW TO LEARN WORDS

1. Use the Study Sheets, Words 1-100.

2. Work from the top to bottom of each page.

3. Write answers in the blanks of each Step.

4. Look back at the top of each Study Sheet to check your answers.

5. It is all right to copy an answer if unsure, because copying correctly helps you learn words.

6. Now, turn the page to begin.

100 STUDY SHEETS

WORD 1 **about**
(a) (bout) 2 syllables

About means **"almost,"** as used in the sentence:

We have **about** an hour until lunch.

STEP 1 <u>**About**</u> means "almost" in:

We have **about** an hour until lunch.

STEP 2 _____ means "almost."

STEP 3 Softly say **about**, and clap once for each one of of the two syllable sounds: **a** and **bout**

STEP 4 Write each syllable in **about**.

_____ _____

STEP 5 Circle or underline **about** in:

We have about an hour until lunch.

STEP 6. "Almost" means:

_____

STEP 7 Fill in the missing letters.

a ____ ____ u t

STEP 8 Complete the sentence by using **about**, which means "almost."

We have _____ thirty minutes until lunch.

STEP 9 You now know how to use **about**, which means "almost."

STEP 10 Write your own sentence using **about**.

_____

_____

_____

_____

> **WORD 2** again
> (a) (gain) 2 syllables
>
> **Again** means **"another time,"** as used in the sentence:
>
> My cousin will come **again** to visit soon.

STEP 1 **Again** means "another time" in:

My cousin will come **again** to visit soon.

STEP 2 _____ means "another time."

STEP 3 Softly say **again**, and clap once for each one of the two syllable sounds: **a** and **gain**

STEP 4 Write each syllable in **again**.

_____   _____

STEP 5 Circle or underline **again** in:

My cousin will come again to visit soon.

STEP 6 "Another time" means:

_____

STEP 7 Fill in the missing letters.

a ____ ____ i n

STEP 8 Complete the sentence by using **again**, which means "another time."

My cousin will come _____ to visit soon.

STEP 9 You now know how to use **again**, which means "another time."

STEP 10 Write your own sentence using **again**.

_____

_____

_____

_____

WORD 3 always
(al) (ways) 2 syllables

Always means **"every time,"** as used in the sentence:

Remember **always** to brush your teeth daily.

STEP 1 **Always** means "every time" in:

Remember **always** to brush your teeth daily.

STEP 2 _____ means "always."

STEP 3 Softly say **always**, and clap once for each one of of the two syllable sounds: **al** and **ways**

STEP 4 Write each syllable in **always**.

_____ _____

STEP 5 Circle or underline **always** in:

Remember always to brush your teeth daily.

STEP 6 "Every time" means:

_____

STEP 7 Fill in the missing letters.

a ____ ____ a y ____

STEP 8 Complete the sentence by using **always**, which means "every time."

Remember _____ to brush your teeth daily.

STEP 9 You now know how to use **always**, which means "every time."

STEP 10 Write your own sentence using **always**.

_____

_____

_____

_____

WORD 4 **another**
(an) (oth) (er) 3 syllables

Another means **"one more,"** as used in the sentence:

I would like **another** piece of pizza.

STEP 1 **Another** means "one more" in:

I would like **another** piece of pizza.

STEP 2 _____ means "one more."

STEP 3 Softly say **another**, and clap once for each one of the three syllable sounds: **an**, **oth**, and **er**

STEP 4 Write each syllable in **another**.

_____ _____ _____

STEP 5 Circle or underline **another** in:

I would like another piece of pizza.

STEP 6 "One more" means:

_____

STEP Fill in the missing letters.

a ____ ____ t h ____ r

STEP 8 Complete the sentence by using **another**, which means "one more."

I would like _____ another piece of pizza.

STEP 9 You now know how to use **another**, which means "one more."

STEP 10 Write your own sentence using **another**.

_____

_____

_____

_____

WORD 5 **anyone**
(an) (y) (one) 3 syllables

Anyone means **"someone not named,"**
as used in the sentence:
Has **anyone** found my backpack?

STEP 1 **Anyone** means "someone not named" in:

Has **anyone** found my backpack?

STEP 2 _____ means "someone not named."

STEP 3 Softly say **anyone**, and clap once for each one of the three syllable sounds: **an, y,** and **one**

STEP 4 Write each syllable in **anyone**.

_____ _____ _____

STEP 5 Circle or underline **anyone** in:

Has anyone found my backpack?

STEP 6 "Someone not named" means:

_____

STEP 7 Fill in the missing letters.

a ___ ___ o ___ e

STEP 8 Complete the sentence by using **anyone** which means "someone not named."

Has _____ found my backpack?

STEP 9 You now know how to use **anyone**, which means "someone not named."

STEP 10 Write your own sentence using **anyone**.

_____

_____

_____

WORD 6   asked
(asked) 1 syllable

Asked means **"questioned,"** as used in the sentence.

Keisha **asked** a friend to visit after school.

STEP 1 **Asked** means "questioned" in:

Keisha **asked** a friend to visit after school.

STEP 2 _____ means "questioned."

STEP 3 Softly say **asked**, and clap once for the one syllable.

STEP 4 Write the one syllable word, **asked**.

_____

STEP 5 Circle or underline **asked** in:

Keisha asked a friend to visit after school.

STEP 6 "Questioned" means:

_____

STEP 7 Fill in the missing letters.

a ____ ____ e d

STEP 8 Complete the sentence by using **asked**, which means "questioned."

Keisha _____ a friend to visit after school.

STEP 9 You now know how to use **asked**, which means "questioned."

STEP 10 Write your own sentence using **asked**.

_____

_____

_____

_____

WORD 7 beautiful
(beau) (ti) (ful) 3 syllables

Beautiful means **"good looking,"**

as used in the sentence:

We saw a **beautiful** sunset.

STEP 1 <u>Beautiful</u> means "good looking" in:

We saw a **beautiful** sunset.

STEP 2 _____ means "good looking."

STEP 3 Softly say **beautiful**, and clap once for each one of the three syllable sounds: **beau, ti**, and **ful**

STEP 4 Write each syllable in **beautiful**.

_____ _____ _____

STEP 5 Circle or underline **beautiful** in:

We saw a beautiful sunset.

STEP 6 "Good looking" means:

_____

STEP 7 Fill in the missing letters.

b ____ ____ u t ____ f ____ l

STEP 8 Complete the sentence by using **beautiful**, which means "good looking."

We saw a _____ sunset.

STEP 9 You now know how to use **beautiful**, which means "good looking."

STEP 10 Write your own sentence using **beautiful**.

_____

_____

_____

_____

WORD 8   **before**
(be) (fore) 2 syllables

Before means **"ahead of,"** as used in the sentence:

We will be home **before** dark.

STEP 1 **Before** means "ahead of" in:

We will be home **before** dark.

STEP 2 _____ means "ahead of."

STEP 3 Softly say **before**, and clap once for each one of the two syllable sounds: **be** and **fore**

STEP 4 Write each syllable in **before**.

_____ _____

STEP 5 Circle or underline **before** in:

We will be home before dark.

STEP 6 "Ahead of" means:

_____

STEP 7 Fill in the missing letters.

b ____ ____ o r ____

STEP 8 Complete the sentence by using **before**, which means "ahead of.

"We will be home _____ dark.

STEP 9 You now know how to use **before**, which means "ahead of."

STEP 10 Write your own sentence using **before**.

_____

_____

_____

_____

WORD 9   **believe**
(be) (lieve) 2 syllables

Believe means **"think it is true,"** as used in the sentence:

My parents could not **believe** that they won a car.

STEP 1 **Believe** means "think it is true" in:

My parents could not **believe** that they won a car.

STEP 2 _____ means "think it is true."

STEP 3 Softly say **believe**, and clap once for each one of the two syllable sounds: **be** and **lieve**

STEP 4 Write each syllable in **believe**.

_____   _____

STEP 5 Circle or underline **believe** in:

My parents could not believe that they won a car.

STEP 6 "Think it is true" means:

_____

STEP 7 Fill in the missing letters.

b ____ l ____ e v ____

STEP 8 Complete the sentence by using **believe** which means "think it is true."

My parents could not _____ that they won a car.

STEP 9 You now know how to use **believe**, which means "think it is true."

STEP 10 Write your own sentence using **believe**.

_____

_____

_____

_____

WORD 10   **best**
(best) 1 syllable

Best means **"finest,"** as used in the sentence:

Try to do your **best** work.

STEP 1 <u>Best</u> means "finest" in:

Try to do your **best** work.

STEP 2 _____ means "finest."

STEP 3 Softly say **best,** and clap once for the one syllable.

STEP 4 Write the one syllable word, **best**.

_____

STEP 5 Circle or underline **best** in:

Try to do your best work.

STEP 6 "Finest" means:

_____

STEP 7 Fill in the missing letters.

b ____ ____ t

STEP 8 Complete the sentence by using **best**, which means "finest."

Try to do your _____ work.

STEP 9 You now know how to use **best**, which means "finest."

STEP 10 Write your own sentence using **best**.

_____

_____

_____

_____

WORD 11 **both**
(both) 1 syllable

Both means **"one and another,"** as used in the sentence:

My sister and I **both** have a game today.

STEP 1 **Both** means "one and another" in:

My sister and I **both** have a game today.

STEP 2 _____ means "one and another."

STEP 3 Softly say **both**, and clap once for the one syllable.

STEP 4 Write the one syllable word, **both**.

_____

STEP 5 Circle or underline **both** in:

My sister and I both have a game today.

STEP 6 "One and another" means:

_____

STEP 7 Fill in the missing letters.

    b _____ t h

STEP 8 Complete the sentence by using **both**, which means "one and another."

My sister and I _____ have a game today.

STEP 9 You now know how to use **both**, which means "one and another."

STEP 10 Write your own sentence using **both**.

_____

_____

_____

_____

WORD 12   **brother**
(broth) (er) 2 syllables

Brother means "boy with same mother or father,"

as used in the sentence:

Lee has one **brother** and one sister.

STEP 1 **Brother** means "boy with same mother or father" in:

Lee has one **brother** and one sister.

STEP 2 _____ means "boy with same

mother or father."

STEP 3 Softly say **brother,** and clap once for each one of the two syllable sounds: **broth** and **er**

STEP 4 Write each syllable in **brother**.

_____ _____

STEP 5 Circle or underline **brother** in:

Lee has one brother and one sister.

STEP 6 "Boy with same mother or father" means:

_____

STEP 7 Fill in the missing letters:

b ____ ____ t ____ e r

STEP 8 Complete the sentence by using **brother**, which means "boy with same mother or father.

Lee has one _____ and one sister.

STEP 9 You now know how to use **brother**, which means "boy with same mother or father."

STEP 10 Write your own sentence using **brother**.

_____

_____

_____

_____

WORD 13 **build**
(build) 1 syllable

Build means "make something,"
as used in the sentence:

Azra is going to **build** a large cage for the rabbit.

STEP 1 **Build** means "make something" in:

Azra is going to **build** a large cage for the rabbit.

STEP 2 _____ means "make something."

STEP 3 Softly say **build**, and clap once for the one syllable.

STEP 4 Write the one syllable word: **build**.

_____

STEP 5 Circle or underline **build** in:

Azra is going to build a large cage for the rabbit.

38

STEP 6 "Make something" means:

_____

STEP 7 Fill in the missing letters.

b ____ ____ l d

STEP 8 Complete the sentence by using **build**, which means "make something."

Azra is going to _____ a large cage for the rabbit.

STEP 9 You now know how to use **build**, which means "make something."

STEP 10 Write your own sentence using **build**.

_____

_____

_____

_____

WORD 14   **busy**
(bus) (y) 2 syllables

Busy means **"active,"** as used in the sentence:

My mother is very **busy** at the computer.

STEP 1 **Busy** means "active" in:

My mother is very **busy** at the computer.

STEP 2 _____ means "active."

STEP 3 Softly say **busy**, and clap once for each one of the two syllable sounds: **bus** and **y**

STEP 4 Write each syllable in **busy**.

_____   _____

STEP 5 Circle or underline **busy** in:

My mother is very busy at the computer.

STEP 6 "Active" means:

_____

STEP 7 Fill in the missing letters.

b ____ ____ y

STEP 8 Complete the sentence by using **busy**, which means "active."

My mother is very _____ at the computer.

STEP 9 You now know how to use **busy**, which means "active."

STEP 10 Write your own sentence using **busy**.

_____

_____

_____

_____

WORD 15 **buy**
(buy) 1 syllable

Buy means **"pay a price for,"** as used in the sentence:

Money can't **buy** happiness.

STEP 1 **Buy** means "pay a price for" in:

Money can't **buy** happiness.

STEP 2 _____ means "pay a price for."

STEP 3 Softly say **buy**, and clap once for the one syllable.

STEP 4 Write the one syllable word, **buy**.

_____

STEP 5 Circle or underline **buy** in:

Money can't buy happiness.

42

STEP 6 "Pay a price for" means:

_____

STEP 7 Fill in the missing letters:

b ____ ____

STEP 8 Complete the sentence by using **buy**, which means "pay a price for."

Money can't _____ happiness.

STEP 9 You now know how to use **buy**, which means "pay a price for."

STEP 10 Write your own sentence using **buy**.

_____

_____

_____

WORD 16 carry
(car) (ry) 2 syllables

Carry means **"hold and move,"** as used in the sentence:

I will **carry** the groceries home.

STEP 1 **Carry** means "hold and move" in:

I will **carry** the groceries home.

STEP 2 _____ means "hold and move."

STEP 3 Softly say **carry**, and clap once for each one of the two syllable sounds: **car** and **ry**

STEP 4 Write each syllable in **carry**.

_____   _____

STEP 5 Circle or underline **carry** in:

I will carry the groceries home.

STEP 6 "Hold and move" means:

_____

STEP 7 Fill in the missing letters

c ____ ____ r y

STEP 8 Complete the sentence by using **carry**, which means "hold and move."

I will _____ the groceries home.

STEP 9 You now know how to use **carry**, which means "hold and move."

STEP 10 Write your own sentence using **carry**.

_____

_____

_____

_____

WORD 17   **caught**
(caught) 1 syllable

Caught means "got something moving,"

as used in the sentence:

I ran and **caught** the ball.

STEP 1   Caught means "got something moving" in:

I ran and **caught** the ball.

STEP 2   _____ means "got something moving."

STEP 3   Softly say **caught**, and clap once for the one syllable.

STEP 4   Write the one syllable word, **caught**.

_____

STEP 5   Circle or underline **caught** in:

I ran and caught the ball.

STEP 6 "Got something moving" means:

_____

STEP 7 Fill in the missing letters.

c ____ ____ g h ____

STEP 8 Complete the sentence by using **caught**, which means "got something moving."

I ran and _____ the ball.

STEP 9 You now know how to use **caught**, which means "got something moving."

STEP 10 Write your own sentence using **caught**.

_____

_____

_____

_____

WORD 18 children
(chil) (dren) 2 syllables

Children means **"young people,"**

as used in the sentence:

Ten **children** play in the school band.

STEP 1 Children means "young people" in:
Ten **children** play in the school band.

STEP 2 _____ means "young people."

STEP 3 Softly say **children**, and clap once for each one of the two syllable sounds: **chil** and **dren**

STEP 4 Write each syllable in **children**.

_____   _____

STEP 5 Circle or underline **children** in:

Ten children play in the school band.

STEP 6 "Young people" means:

_____

STEP 7 Fill in the missing letters.

c ____ ____ l d ____ e n

STEP 8 Complete the sentence by using **children**, which means "young people."

Ten _____ play in the school band.

STEP 9 You now know how to use **children**, which means "young people."

STEP 10 Write your own sentence using **children**.

_____

_____

_____

WORD 19   **city**
(ci) (ty) 2 syllables

City means **"where many people live,"**
as used in the sentence:

A **city** has more people than a town.

STEP 1 **City** means "where many people live" in:
A **city** has more people than a town.

STEP 2 _____ means "where many people live."

STEP 3 Softly say **city**, and clap once for each one of the two syllable sounds: **ci** and **ty**

STEP 4 Write each syllable in **city**.

_____ _____

STEP 5 Circle or underline **city** in:

A city has more people than a town.

STEP 6 "Where many people live" means:

_____

STEP 7 Fill in the missing letters.

c ____ ____ y

STEP 8 Complete the sentence by using **city**, which means "where many people live."

A _____ has more people than a town.

STEP 9 You now know how to use **city**, which means "where many people live."

STEP 10 Write your own sentence using **city**.

_____

_____

_____

_____

WORD 20   **could**
(could) 1 syllable

Could means **"was able to,"** as used in the sentence:

I didn't know Nan **could** play the drums.

STEP 1 **Could** means "was able to" in:

I didn't know Nan **could** play the drums.

STEP 2 _____ means "was able to."

STEP 3 Softly say **could**, and clap once for the one syllable.

STEP 4 Write the one syllable word, **could**.

_____

STEP 5 Circle or underline **could** in:

I didn't know Nan could play the drums.

STEP 6 "Was able to" means:

_____

STEP 7 Fill in the missing letters.

c ____ ____ l d

STEP 8 Complete the sentence by using **could**, which means "was able to."

I didn't know Nan _____ play drums.

STEP 9 You now know how to use **could**, which means "was able to."

STEP 10 Write your own sentence using **could**.

_____

_____

_____

_____

WORD 21   **country**
(coun) (try) 2 syllables

Country means "land outside cities and towns,"
as used in the sentence:
The mouse from the **country** does not like the city.

STEP 1 **Country** means "land outside cities and towns" in:

The mouse from the **country** does not like the city.

STEP 2 _____ means "land outside cities and towns."

STEP 3 Softly say **country**, and clap once for each one of the two syllable sounds: **coun** and **try**

STEP 4 Write each syllable in **country**.

_____ _____

STEP 5 Circle or underline **country** in:

The mouse from the country does not like the city.

STEP 6 "Land outside cities and towns" means:

_____

STEP 7 Fill in the missing letters.

c ____ ____ n t ____ y

STEP 8 Complete the sentence by using **country**, which means "land outside cities and towns."

The mouse from the_____ does not like the city.

STEP 9 You now know how to use **country**, which means "land outside cities and towns."

STEP 10 Write your own sentence using **country**.

_____

_____

_____

_____

WORD 22   cousin
(cous) (in) 2 syllables

Cousin means **"child of aunt or uncle,"**
as used in the sentence:
I have one **cousin** whose mother is my Aunt Ann.

STEP 1   **Cousin** means "child of aunt or uncle" in:

I have one **cousin** whose mother is my Aunt Ann.

STEP 2   _____ means "child of aunt or uncle."

STEP 3   Softly say **cousin**, and clap once for each one of the two syllable sounds: **cous** and **in**

STEP 4   Write each syllable in **cousin**.

_____ _____

STEP 5   Circle or underline **cousin** in:

I have one cousin whose mother is my Aunt Ann.

STEP 6 "Child of aunt or uncle " means:

_____

STEP 7 Fill in the missing letters.

c ____ ____ s ____ n

STEP 8 Complete the sentence by using **cousin**, which means "child of aunt or uncle."

I have one _____ whose mother is my Aunt Ann.

STEP 9 You now know how to use **cousin**, which means "child of aunt or uncle."

STEP 10 Write your own sentence using **cousin**.

_____

_____

_____

_____

WORD 23 **dear**
(dear) 1 syllable

Dear means **"loved,"** as used in the sentence:

"**Dear** Dan," began the letter.

STEP 1 **Dear** means "loved" in:

"**Dear** Dan," began the letter.

STEP 2 _____ means "loved."

STEP 3 Softly say **dear**, and clap once for the one syllable.

STEP 4 Write the one syllable word, **dear**.

_____

STEP 5 Circle or underline **dear** in:

"Dear Dan," began the letter

STEP 6 "Loved" means:

_____

STEP 7 Fill in the missing letters.

d ____ ____ r

STEP 8 Complete the sentence by using **dear**, which means "loved."

"_____ Dan," began the letter.

STEP 9 You now can use **dear**, which means "loved."

STEP 10 Write your own sentence using **dear**.

_____

_____

_____

_____

WORD 24 **didn't**
(did) (n't) 2 syllables

Didn't means **"did not,"** as used in the sentence:

Jake **didn't** knock before going into the house.

STEP 1 **Didn't** means "did not" in:

Jake **didn't** knock before going into the house.

STEP 2 _____ means "did not."

STEP 3 Softly say **didn't**, and clap once for each one of the two syllable sounds: **did** and **n't**

STEP 4 Write each syllable in **didn't**.

_____   _____

STEP 5 Circle or underline **didn't** in:

Jake didn't knock before going into the house.

STEP 6 "Did not" means:

_____

STEP 7 Fill in the missing letters.

d ____ ____ n ' ____

STEP 8 Complete the sentence by using **didn't**, which means "did not."

Jake _____ knock before going into the house.

STEP 9 You now know how to use **didn't**, which means "did not."

STEP 10 Write your own sentence using **didn't**.

_____

_____

_____

_____

WORD 25   **different**
(dif) (fer) (ent)   3 syllables

Different means **"not the same,"**
as used in the sentence:

Dogs and cats are **different**.

STEP 1 **Different** means "not the same" in:

Dogs and cats are **different**.

STEP 2 _____ means "not the same."

STEP 3 Softly say **different** and clap once for each one of the three syllable sounds: **dif, fer,** and **ent**

STEP 4 Write each syllable in **different**.

_____ _____ _____

STEP 5 Circle or underline **different** in:

Dogs and cats are different.

STEP 6 "Not the same" means:

_____

STEP 7 Fill in the missing letters.

d ____ ____ f ____ r e ____ t

STEP 8 Complete the sentence by using **different**, which means "different."

Dogs and cats are _____.

STEP 9 You now know how to use **different**, which means "not the same."

STEP 10 Write your own sentence using **different**.

_____

_____

_____

_____

WORD 26   **does**

(does) 1 syllable

Does means **"performs,"** as used in the sentence:

Our class **does** good work.

STEP 1 **Does** means "performs" in:

Our class **does** good work.

STEP 2 _____ means "performs."

STEP 3 Softly say **does**, and clap once for the one syllable.

STEP 4 Write the one syllable word, **does**.

_____

STEP 5 Circle or underline **does** in:

Our class does good work.

STEP 6 "Performs" means:

_____

STEP 7 Fill in the missing letters.

d ____ ____ s

STEP 8 Complete the sentence by using **does**, which means "performs."

Our class _____ good work.

STEP 9 You now know how to use **does**, which means "performs."

STEP 10 Write your own sentence using **does**.

_____

_____

_____

WORD 27 **doesn't**
(does) (n't) 2 syllables

Doesn't means **"does not,"** as used in the sentence:

My friend **doesn't** want to go shopping today.

STEP 1 **Doesn't** means "does not" in:

My friend **doesn't** want to go shopping today.

STEP 2 _____ means "does not."

STEP 3 Softly say **doesn't**, and clap once for each one of the two syllable sounds: **does** and **n't**.

STEP 4 Write each syllable in **doesn't**.

_____ _____

STEP 5 Circle or underline **doesn't** in:

My friend doesn't want to go shopping today.

STEP 6 "Doesn't" means:

_____

STEP 7 Fill in the missing letters.

d ____ ____ s ____ ' t

STEP 8 Complete the sentence by using **doesn't**, which means "does not."

My friend _____ want to go shopping today.

STEP 9 You now know how to use **doesn't**, which means "does not."

STEP 10 Write your own sentence using **doesn't**.

_____

_____

_____

_____

WORD 28 done
(done) 1 syllable

Done means **"finished,"** as used in the sentence:

Have you **done** your homework?

STEP 1 **Done** means "finished" in:

Have you **done** your homework?

STEP 2 _____ means "finished."

STEP 3 Softly say **done**, and clap once for the one syllable.

STEP 4 Write the one syllable word, **done.**

_____

STEP 5 Circle or underline **done** in:

Have you done your homework?

STEP 6 "Finished" means:

_____

STEP 7 Fill in the missing letters.

d ____ ____ e

STEP 8 Complete the sentence by using **done**, which means "finished."

Have you _____ your homework.

STEP 9 You now can know how to use **done**, which means "finished."

STEP 10 Write your own sentence using **done**.

_____

_____

_____

_____

WORD 29   **door**
(door) 1 syllable

Door means **"something that closes off space,"**

as used in the sentence:

A locked **door** opens with a key.

STEP 1   Door means "something that closes off space" in:
A locked **door** opens with a key.

STEP 2   _____ means "something that closes off space."

STEP 3   Softly say **door**, and clap once for the one syllable.

STEP 4   Write the one syllable word, **door**.

_____

STEP 5   Circle or underline **door** in:

A locked door opens with a key.

STEP 6 "Something that closes off space" means:

_____

STEP 7 Fill in the missing letters

d ____ ____ r

STEP 8 Complete the sentence by using **door** which means "something that closes off space."

A locked _____ opens with a key.

STEP 9 You now know how to use **door**, which means "something that closes off space."

STEP 10 Write your own sentence using **door**.

_____

_____

_____

_____

WORD 30 **drink**

(drink) 1 syllable

Drink means **"swallow liquid,"** as used in the sentence:

My baby sister will **drink** all of the milk.

STEP 1 <u>Drink</u> means "swallow liquid" in:

My baby sister will **drink** all of the milk.

STEP 2 _____ means "swallow liquid."

STEP 3 Softly say **drink**, and clap once for the one syllable.

STEP 4 Write the one syllable word, **drink**.

_____ 4

STEP 5 Circle or underline **drink** in:

My baby sister will drink all of the milk.

STEP 6 "Swallow liquid" means:

_____

STEP 7 Fill in the missing letters.

d ____ ____ n k

STEP 8 Complete the sentence by using **drink**, which means "swallow liquid."

My baby sister will _____ all of the milk.

STEP 9 You now know how to use **drink**, which means "swallow liquid."

STEP 10 Write your own sentence using **drink**.

_____

_____

_____

_____

WORD 31 **drop**
(drop) 1 syllable

Drop means **"let fall,"** as used in the sentence:

I don't want to **drop** my ice-cream cone.

STEP 1 **Drop** means "let fall" in:

I don't want to **drop** my ice-cream cone.

STEP 2 _____ means "let fall."

STEP 3 Softly say **drop**, and clap once for the one syllable.

STEP 4 Write the one syllable word, **drop**.

_____

STEP 5 Circle or underline **drop** in:

I don't want to drop my ice-cream cone.

STEP 6 "Let fall" means:

_____

STEP 7 Fill in the missing letters.

d ____ ____ p

STEP 8 Complete the sentence by using **drop**, which means "let fall."

I don't want to _____ my ice-cream cone.

STEP 9 You now know how to use **drop**, which means "let fall."

STEP 10 Write your own sentence using **drop**.

_____

_____

_____

_____

> **WORD 32**   **easy**
> (ea) (sy) **2 syllables**
>
> **Easy** means **"not hard to do,"** as used in the sentence:
>
> It is **easy** to read with my new glasses.

STEP 1 <u>Easy</u> means "not hard to do" in:

    It is **easy** to read with my new glasses.

STEP 2 _____ means "not hard to do."

STEP 3 Softly say **easy**, and clap while saying each one of the two syllable sounds: **ea** and **sy**

STEP 4 Write each syllable in **easy**:

    _____ _____

STEP 5 Circle or underline **easy** in:

    It is easy to read with my new glasses.

STEP 6 "Not hard to do" means:

_____

STEP 7 Fill in the missing letters.

e ____ ____ y

STEP 8 Complete the sentence by using **easy**, which means "not hard to do."

It's _____ to read with my new glasses.

STEP 9 You now know how to use **easy**, which means "not hard to do."

STEP 10 Write your own sentence using **easy**.

_____

_____

_____

_____

WORD 33   **enough**
(e) (nough) 2 syllables

Enough means **"as much as needed,"**

as used in the sentence:

We have **enough** food for the party.

STEP 1 **Enough** means "as much as needed" in:

We have **enough** food for the party.

STEP 2 _____ means "as much as needed."

STEP 3 Softly say **enough**, and clap while saying each one of the two syllable sounds: **e** and **nough**

STEP 4 Write each syllable in **enough**.

_____ _____

STEP 5 Circle or underline **enough** in:

We have enough food for the party.

STEP 6 "As much as needed" means:

_____

STEP 7 Fill in the missing letters.

e ____ ____ u ____ h

STEP 8 Complete the sentence by using enough which means "as much as needed."

We have _____ food for the party.

STEP 9 You now know how to use **enough**, which means "as much as needed."

STEP 10 Write your own sentence using **enough**.

_____

_____

_____

_____

WORD 34 **every**
(e) (ver) (y) 3 syllables

Every means **"all in a group,"** as used in the sentence:

Every student went on the class trip.

STEP 1 **Every** means "all in a group" in:

Every student went on the class trip.

STEP 2 _____ means "all in a group."

STEP 3 Softly say **every**, and clap once for each one of the three syllable sounds: **e, ver,** and **ry**

STEP 4 Write each syllable in **every**.

_____   _____   _____

STEP 5 Circle or underline **every** in:

Every student went on the class trip.

80

STEP 6 "All in a group" means:

_____

STEP 7 Fill in the missing letters.

e v ____ r ____

STEP 8 Complete the sentence by using enough which means "all in a group."

_____ student went on the class trip.

STEP 9 You now know how to use **every**, which means "all in a group."

STEP 10 Write your own sentence using **every**.

_____

_____

_____

_____

> **WORD 35** eye
> (eye) 1 syllable
>
> **Eye means "body part for seeing,"**
> as used in the sentence:
>
> I can close one **eye** at a time.

STEP 1 <u>Eye</u> means "body part for seeing" in:

I can close one **eye** at a time.

STEP 2 _____ means "body part for seeing."

STEP 3 Softly say **eye**, and clap once for the one syllable.

STEP 4 Write the one syllable word, **eye**.

_____

STEP 5 Circle or underline **eye** in:

I can close one eye at a time

STEP 6 "Body part for seeing" means:

_____

STEP 7 Fill in the missing letter.

e ____ e

STEP 8 Complete the sentence by using **eye**, which means "body part for seeing."

I can close one _____ at a time.

STEP 9 You now know how to use **eye**, which means "body part for seeing."

STEP 10 Write your own sentence using **eye**.

_____

_____

_____

_____

WORD 36 face
(face) 1 syllable

Face means "**front part of the head**,"
as used in the sentence:

My nose and eyes are on my **face**.

STEP 1 <u>Face</u> means "front part of the head" in:

My nose and eyes are on my **face**.

STEP 2 _____ means "front part of the head."

STEP 3 Softly say **face**, and clap once for the one syllable.

STEP 4 Write the one syllable word, **face**.

_____

STEP 5 Circle or underline **face** in:

My nose and eyes are on my face.

STEP 6 "Front part of the head" means:

_____

STEP 7 Fill in the missing letters.

f ____ ____ e

STEP 8 Complete the sentence by using **face**, which means "front part of the head."

My nose and eyes are on my _____.

STEP 9 Now you know how to use **face**, which means "front part of the head."

STEP 10 Write your own sentence using **face**.

_____

_____

_____

_____

WORD 37   first
(first) 1 syllable

First means "**before all else**," as used in the sentence:

A is the **first** letter in the alphabet.

STEP 1   **First** means "before all else" in:

A is the **first** letter in the alphabet.

STEP 2   _____ means "before all else."

STEP 3   Softly say **first**, and clap once for the one syllable.

STEP 4   Write the one syllable word, **first**.

_____

STEP 5   Circle or underline **first** in:

A is the first letter in the alphabet.

STEP 6 "Before all else" means:

_____

STEP 7 Fill in the missing letters.

f ____ ____ s t

STEP 8 Complete the sentence by using **first**, which means "before all else."

A is the _____ letter of the alphabet.

STEP 9 Now you know how to use **first**, which means "before all else."

STEP 10 Write your own sentence using **first**.

_____

_____

_____

_____

WORD 38 **forty**

(for) (ty) **2 syllables**

Forty means **"the number 40,"** as used in the sentence:

Our food market has over **forty** ice cream flavors.

STEP 1 <u>Forty</u> means "the number 40" in:

Our food market has over **forty** ice cream flavors.

STEP 2 _____ means "the number 40."

STEP 3 Softly say **forty**, and clap once for each one of the two syllable sounds: **for** and **ty**

STEP 4 Write the one syllable word: **forty**.

_____

STEP 5 Circle or underline **forty** in:

Our food market has over forty ice cream flavors.

STEP 6 "The number 40" means:

_____

STEP 7 Fill in the missing letters.

f ____ ____ t ____

STEP 8 Complete the sentence by using **forty**, which means "the number 40."

Our food market has over _____ ice cream flavors.

STEP 9 Now you know how to use **forty**, which means "the number 40."

STEP 10 Write your own sentence using **forty**.

_____

_____

_____

_____

WORD 39   **girl**
(girl) **1 syllable**

Girl means **"female child,"** as used in the sentence:

I met the new **girl** in our class.

STEP 1 <u>Girl</u> means "female child" in:

I met the new **girl** in our class.

STEP 2 _____ means "female child."

STEP 3 Softly say **girl**, and clap once for the one syllable.

STEP 4 Write the one syllable word, **girl**.

_____

STEP 5 Circle or underline **girl** in:

I met the new girl in our class.

STEP 6 "Female child" means:

_____

STEP 7 Fill in the missing letters:

g ____ ____ l

STEP 8 Complete the sentence by using **girl**, which means "female child."

I met the new _____ in our class.

STEP 9 Now you know how to use **girl**, which means "female child."

STEP 10 Write your own sentence using **girl**.

_____

_____

_____

_____

> **WORD 40** **give**
> (give) 1 syllable
>
> **Give** means "**let have**," as used in the sentence:
>
> I would like to **give** you a special present.

STEP 1 <u>Give</u> means "let have" in:

I would like to **give** you a special present.

STEP 2 _____ means "let have."

STEP 3 Softly say **give**, and clap once for the one syllable.

STEP 4 Write the one syllable word, **give**.

_____

STEP 5 Circle or underline **give** in:

I would like to give you a special present.

STEP 6 "Let have" means:

_____

STEP 7 Fill in the missing letters.

g ____ ____ e

STEP 8 Complete the sentence by using **give**, which means "let have."

I would like to _____ you a special present.

STEP 9 Now you how to use **give**, which means "let have."

STEP 10 Write your own sentence using **give**.

_____

_____

_____

_____

WORD 41   **good**
(good) 1 syllable

Good means **"very fine,"** as used in the sentence:

My apple tastes **good**.

STEP 1 **Good** means "very fine" in:

My apple tastes **good.**

STEP 2 _____ means "very fine."

STEP 3 Softly say **good**, and clap once for the one syllable.

STEP 4 Write the one syllable word, **good**.

_____

STEP 5 Circle or underline **good** in:

My apple tastes good.

STEP 6 "Very fine" means:

_____

STEP 7 Fill in the missing letters.

g ____ ____ d

STEP 8 Complete the sentence by using **good**, which means "very fine."

My apple tastes _____.

STEP 9 Now you know how to use **good**, which means "very fine."

STEP 10 Write your own sentence using **good**.

_____

_____

_____

_____

WORD 42   **great**
(great) 1 syllable

Great means **"very good,"** as used in the sentence:

I had a great time at my new school today.

STEP 1 <u>Great</u> means "very good" in:

I had a **great** time at my new school today.

STEP 2 _____ means "very good."

STEP 3 Softly say **great**, and clap once for the one syllable.

STEP 4 Write the one syllable word, **great**.

_____

STEP 5 Circle or underline **great** in:

I had a great time at my new school today.

STEP 6 "Very good" means:

_____

STEP 7 Fill in the missing letters.

g ____ ____ a t

STEP 8 Complete the sentence by using **great**, which means "very good."

I had a _____ time at school today.

STEP 9 Now you know how to use **great**, which means "very good."

STEP 10 Write your own sentence using **great**.

_____

_____

_____

_____

WORD 43   have
(have) 1 syllable

Have means **"own,"** as used in the sentence:

We want our team to **have** new shirts.

STEP 1 **Have** means "own" in:

We want our team to **have** new shirts.

STEP 2 _____ means "own."

STEP 3 Softly say **have**, and clap once for the one syllable.

STEP 4 Write the one syllable word, **have**.

_____

STEP 5 Circle or underline **have** in:

We want our team to have new shirts.

STEP 6 "Own" means:

_____

STEP 7 Fill in the missing letters.

h ____ ____ e

STEP 8 Complete the sentence by using **have**, which means "own."

We want our team to _____ new shirts.

STEP 9 You now know how to use **have**, which means "own."

STEP 10 Write your own sentence using **have**.

_____

_____

_____

_____

WORD 44   **head**
(head) 1 syllable

Head means "body part above the neck,"
as used in the sentence:

Eyes, ears, nose and mouth are all part of the **head**.

STEP 1 **Head** means "body part above the neck" in:

Eyes, ears, nose and mouth are all part of the **head**.

STEP 2 _____ means "body part above the neck."

STEP 3 Softly say **head**, and clap once for the one syllable.

STEP 4 Write the one syllable word, **head**.

_____

STEP 5 Circle or underline **head** in:

Eyes, ears, nose and mouth are all part of the head.

STEP 6 "Body part above the neck" means:

_____

STEP 7 Fill in the missing letters.

h ____ ____ d

STEP 8 Complete the sentence by using **head**, which means "body part above the neck.

Eyes, ears, nose and mouth are all part of the _____.

STEP 9 You now know how to use **head** which means "body part above the neck."

STEP 10 Write your own sentence using **head**.

_____

_____

_____

_____

WORD 45 heard
(heard) 1 syllable

Heard means **"listened to,"** as used in the sentence:

I **heard** the thunder before the storm.

STEP 1 **Heard** means "listened to" in:

I **heard** the thunder before the storm.

STEP 2 _____ means "listened to."

STEP 3 Softly say **heard**, and clap once for the one syllable.

STEP 4 Write the one syllable word, **heard**.

_____

STEP 5 Circle or underline **heard** in:

I heard the thunder before the storm

STEP 6 "Listened to" means:

_____

STEP 7 Fill in the missing letters.

h ____ ____ r d

STEP 8 Complete the sentence by using **heard**, which means listened to."

I _____ the thunder before the storm.

STEP 9 You now know how to use **heard**, which means "listened to."

STEP 10 Write your own sentence using **heard**.

_____

_____

_____

_____

WORD 46 **here**
(here) 1 syllable

Here means **"where you are now,"**

as used in the sentence:

My cat, Fluff, is **here** in the kitchen.

STEP 1 **Here** means "where you are now" in:

My cat, Fluff, is **here** in the kitchen.

STEP 2 _____ means "where you are now."

STEP 3 Softly say **here**, and clap once for the one syllable.

STEP 4 Write the one syllable word, **here**.

_____

STEP 5 Circle or underline **here** in:

My cat, Fluff, is here in the kitchen.

STEP 6 "Where you are now" means:

_____

STEP 7 Fill in the missing letters.

h ____ ____ e

STEP 8 Complete the sentence by using **here**, which means "where you are now."

My cat, Fluff, is _____ in the kitchen.

STEP 9 You now can use **here**, which means "where you are now."

STEP 10 Write your own sentence using **here**.

_____

_____

_____

_____

> **WORD 47** house
> (house) 1 syllable
>
> **House means "building where people live,"**
> as used in the sentence:
>
> We have two families living in our **house**.

STEP 1 <u>House</u> means "building where people live" in:

We have two families living in our **house**.

STEP 2 _____ means "building where people live."

STEP 3 Softly say **house**, and clap once for the one syllable.

STEP 4 Write the one syllable word, **house**.

_____

STEP 5 Circle or underline **house** in:

We have two families living in our house.

STEP 6 "Building where people live" means:

_____

STEP 7 Fill in the missing letters.

h ____ ____ s e

STEP 8 Complete the sentence by using **house**, which means "building where people live."

We have two families living in our _____.

STEP 9 You now know how to use **house**, which means "building where people live."

STEP 10 Write your own sentence using **house**.

_____

_____

_____

_____

WORD 48   **hurt**
(hurt) 1 syllable

Hurt means "have a feeling of pain,"
as used in the sentence:

The flu shot didn't **hurt**.

STEP 1 <u>Hurt</u> means "have a feeling of pain" in:

The flu shot didn't **hurt.**

STEP 2 _____ means "have a feeling of pain."

STEP 3 Softly say **hurt**, and clap once for the one syllable.

STEP 4 Write the one syllable word, **hurt**.

_____

STEP 5 Circle or underline **hurt** in:

The flu shot didn't hurt.

STEP 6 "Have a feeling of pain" means:

_____

STEP 7 Fill in the missing letters.

h ____ ____ t

STEP 8 Complete the sentence by using **hurt**, which means "have a feeling of pain.

The flu shot didn't _____.

STEP 9 You now know how to use **hurt**, which means "have a feeling of pain."

STEP 10 Write your own sentence using **hurt**.

_____

_____

_____

_____

WORD 49 idea
(i) (dea) 2 syllables

Idea means **"thought,"** as used in the sentence:

What a good **idea** to take our umbrella on this rainy day!

STEP 1 <u>Idea</u> means "thought" in:

What a good **idea** to take our umbrella on this rainy day!

STEP 2 _____ means "thought."

STEP 3 Softly say **idea**, and clap once for each one of the two syllable sounds: **i** and **dea**

STEP 4 Write each syllable in **idea**.

_____ _____

STEP 5 Circle or underline **idea** in:

What a good idea to take our umbrella on this rainy day!

STEP 6 "Thought " means:

_____

STEP 7 Fill in the missing letters.

I ____ ____ a

STEP 8 Complete the sentence by using **idea**, which means "thought.

What a good _____ to take our umbrella on this rainy day.

STEP 9 You now know how to use **idea**, which means "thought."

STEP 10 Write your own sentence using **idea**.

_____

_____

_____

_____

WORD 50   it's
(it's) 1 syllable

It's means **"it is,"** as used in the sentence:

It's a good day in the neighborhood.

STEP 1 **It's** means "it is" in:

It's a good day in the neighborhood.

STEP 2 _____ means "it is."

STEP 3 Softly say **it's**, and clap once for the one syllable.

STEP 4 Write the one syllable word, **it's**.

_____

STEP 5 Circle or underline **it's** in:

It's a good day in the neigborhood.

STEP 6 "It is" means:

_____

STEP 7 Fill in the missing letter.

i ____ ' s

STEP 8 Complete the sentence by using **it's**, which means "it is."

_____ a good day in the neighborhood.

STEP 9 You now know how to use **it's**, which means "it is."

STEP 10 Write your own sentence using **it's**.

_____

_____

_____

_____

WORD 51 knew
(knew) 1 syllable

Knew means **"was sure of,"** as used in the sentence:

I **knew** all the answers on the test.

STEP 1 **Knew** means "was sure of" in:

I **knew** all the answers on the test.

STEP 2 _____ means "was sure of."

STEP 3 Softly say **knew**, and clap once for the one syllable.

STEP 4 Write the one syllable word, **knew**.

_____

STEP 5 Circle or underline **knew** in:

I knew all the answers on the test.

STEP 6 "Was sure of" means:

_____

STEP 7 Fill in the missing letters.

k ____ ____ w

STEP 8 Complete the sentence by using **knew**, which means "was sure of."

I _____ all the answers on the test.

STEP 9 You now know how to use knew, which means "was sure of."

STEP 10 Write your own sentence using **knew**.

_____

_____

_____

_____

WORD 52   **large**
(large) 1 syllable

Large means **"big,"** as used in the sentence:

Whales are **large** animals.

STEP 1 **Large** means "big" in:

Whales are **large** animals.

STEP 2 _____ means "big."

STEP 3 Softly say **large**, and clap once for the one syllable.

STEP 4 Write the one syllable word, **large**.

_____

STEP 5 Circle or underline **large** in:

Whales are large animals.

STEP 6 "Big" means:

_____

STEP 7 Fill in the missing letters.

l ____ ____ g e

STEP 8 Complete the sentence by using **large**, which means "big."

Whales are _____ animals.

STEP 9 You now know how to use **large**, which means "big."

STEP 10 Write your own sentence using **large**.

_____

_____

_____

_____

> **WORD 53**   **light**
> (light) **1 syllable**
>
> **Light** means **"lamp for seeing,"** as used in the sentence:
>
> Barbara turned on the **light** to read the book.

STEP 1 <u>Light</u> means "lamp for seeing" in:

    Barbara turned on the **light** to read the book.

STEP 2 _____ means "lamp for seeing."

STEP 3 Softly say **light**, and clap once for the one syllable.

STEP 4 Write the one syllable word, **light**.

_____

STEP 5 Circle or underline **light** in:

    Barbara turned on the light to read the book.

STEP 6 "Lamp for seeing" means:

_____

STEP 7 Fill in the missing letters.

l ____ ____ h t

STEP 8 Complete the sentence by using **light**, which means "lamp for seeing."

Barbara turned on the _____ to read the book.

STEP 9 You now know how to use **light**, which means "lamp for seeing."

STEP 10 Write your own sentence using **light**.

_____

_____

_____

_____

WORD 54   **listen**
(lis) (ten) 2 syllables

Listen means **"hear carefully,"** as used in the sentence:

Janna loves to **listen** to music.

STEP 1   <u>Listen</u> means "hear carefully" in:

Janna loves to **listen** to music.

STEP 2   _____ means "hear carefully."

STEP 3   Softly say **listen**, and clap once for each one of the two syllable sounds: **lis** and **ten**

STEP 4   Write each syllable in **listen**.

_____ _____

STEP 5   Circle or underline **listen** in:

Janna loves to listen to music.

STEP 6 "Hear carefully" means:

_____

STEP 7 Fill in the missing letters.

l ____ ____ t ____ n

STEP 8 Complete the sentence by using **listen**, which means "hear carefully."

Janna loves to _____ to music.

STEP 9 You now know how to use **listen**, which means "hear carefully."

STEP 10 Write your own sentence using **listen**.

_____

_____

_____

WORD 55   **look**
(look) 1 syllable

Look means **"use eyes to see,"** as used in the sentence:

Look at the **beautiful** sunset.

STEP 1 **Look** means "use eyes to see" in:

       Look at the beautiful sunset.

STEP 2 _____ means "use eyes to see."

STEP 3 Softly say **look**, and clap once for the one syllable.

STEP 4 Write the one syllable word, **look**.

       _____

STEP 5 Circle or underline **look** in:

       Look at the beautiful sunset.

STEP 6 "Use eyes to see" means:

_____

STEP 7 Fill in the missing letters.

l ____ ____ k

STEP 8 Complete the sentence by using **look**, which means "use eyes to see."

_____ at the beautiful sunset.

STEP 9 You now know how to use **look**, which means "use eyes to see."

STEP 10 Write your own sentence using **look**.

_____

_____

_____

_____

WORD 56 mail
(mail) 1 syllable

Mail means "sent, as by the post office,"
as used in the sentence:

I got the **mail** in our mailbox.

STEP 1 **Mail** means "sent, as by the post office" in:

I got the **mail** in our mailbox.

STEP 2 _____ means "sent, as by the post office."

STEP 3 Softly say **mail**, and clap once for the one syllable.

STEP 4 Write the one syllable word, **mail**.

_____

STEP 5 Circle or underline **mail** in:

I got the mail in our mailbox.

STEP 6 "Sent, as by the post office" means:

_____

STEP 7 Fill in the missing letters.

m ____ ____ l

STEP 8 Complete the sentence by using **mail**, which means "sent, as by the post office."

I got the _____ in our mailbox.

STEP 9 You now know how to use **mail**, which means "sent, as by the post office."

STEP 10 Write your own sentence using **mail**.

_____
_____
_____
_____

WORD 57   **make**
(make) 1 syllable

Make means **"put together,"** as used in the sentence:

Manny will **make** dinner tonight.

STEP 1 **Make** means "put together" in:

Manny will **make** dinner tonight.

STEP 2 _____ means "put together."

STEP 3 Softly say **make**, and clap once for the one syllable.

STEP 4 Write the one syllable word, **make**.

_____

STEP 5 Circle or underline **make** in:

Manny will make dinner tonight.

STEP 6 "Put together" means:

_____

STEP 7 Fill in the missing letters.

m ____ ____ e

STEP 8 Complete the sentence by using **make**, which means "put together."

Manny will _____ dinner tonight.

STEP 9 You now know how to use **make**, which means "put together."

STEP 10 Write your own sentence using **make**.

_____

_____

_____

_____

> **WORD 58**   **many**
> (man) (y) 2 syllables
>
> **Many** means **"a large number of,"** as used in the sentence:
>
>   <u>**Many**</u> people have cell phones.

STEP 1   <u>**Many**</u> means "a large number of" in:

           <u>**Many**</u> people have cell phones.

STEP 2   _____ means "a large number of."

STEP 3   Softly say **many**, and clap once for each one of the two syllable sounds: **man** and **y**

STEP 4   Write each syllable in **many**.

           _____ _____

STEP 5   Circle or underline **many** in:

           Many people have cell phones.

STEP 6 "A large number of" means:

_____

STEP 7 Fill in the missing letters.

m ____ ____ y

STEP 8 Complete the sentence by using **many**, which means "a large number of."

_____ people have cell phones.

STEP 9 You now know how to use **many**, which means "a large number of."

STEP 10 Write your own sentence using **many**.

_____

_____

_____

_____

> **WORD 59**   **measure**
> **(meas) (ure) 2 syllables**
>
> **Measure means "find out the size of,"**
> as used in the sentence:
>
> Hanna helped me **measure** the room.

STEP 1 **Measure** means "find out the size of" in:

    Hanna helped me **measure** the room.

STEP 2 _____ means "find out the size of."

STEP 3 Softly say **measure**, and clap once for each one of the two syllable sounds: **meas** and **ure**

STEP 4 Write each syllable in **measure**.

    _____ _____

STEP 5 Circle or underline **measure** in:

    Hanna helped me measure the room.

STEP 6 "Find out the size of" means:

_____

STEP 7 Fill in the missing letters.

m ____ ____ s ____ r e

STEP 8 Complete the sentence by using **measure** which means "find out the size of."

Hanna helped me _____ the room.

STEP 9 You now know how to use **measure**, which means "find out the size of."

STEP 10 Write your own sentence using **measure**.

_____

_____

_____

_____

WORD 60　　　　more
(more) 1 syllable

More means **"a larger number"** as used in the sentence:

We have **more than** 20 pens.

STEP 1 **More** means "a larger number" in:

We have **more than** 20 pens.

STEP 2 _____ means "a larger number."

STEP 3 Softly say **more**, and clap once for the one syllable.

STEP 4 Write the one syllable word, **more**.

_____

STEP 5 Circle or underline **more** in:

We have more than 20 pens.

STEP 6 "A larger number" means:

_____

STEP 7 Fill in the missing letters.

m ____ ____ e

STEP 8 Complete the sentence by using **more**, which means "a larger number."

We have _____ than 20 pens.

STEP 9 You now know how to use **more**, which means "a larger number."

STEP 10 Write your own sentence using **more**.

_____

_____

_____

_____

> **WORD 61** **often**
> (of) (ten) 2 syllables
>
> **Often** means **"many times,"** as used in the sentence:
>
> We go to the park **often** in the summer.

STEP 1 **Often** means "many times" in:

　　We go to the park **often** in the summer.

STEP 2 _____ means "many times."

STEP 3 Softly say **often**, and clap once for each one of the two syllable sounds: **of** and **ten**

STEP 4 Write each syllable in **often**.

　　_____   _____

STEP 5 Circle or underline **often** in:

　　We go to the park often in the summer.

STEP 6 "Many times" means:

_____

STEP 7 Fill in the missing letters.

o ____ ____ e n

STEP 8 Complete the sentence by using **often**, which means "many times."

We go to the park _____ in the summer.

STEP 9 You now know how to use often, which means "many times."

STEP 10 Write your own sentence using **often**.

_____

_____

_____

_____

WORD 62 **once**
(once) 1 syllable

Once means **"one time,"** as used in the sentence:

I went only **once** to the zoo.

STEP 1 **Once** means "one time" in:

I went only **once** to the zoo.

STEP 2 _____ means "one time."

STEP 3 Softly say **once**, and clap once for the one syllable.

STEP 4 Write the one syllable word, **once**.

_____

STEP 5 Circle or underline **once** in:

I went only once to the zoo.

STEP 6 "One time" means:

_____

STEP 7 Fill in the missing letters.

o ____ ____ e

STEP 8 Complete the sentence by using **once**, which means "one time."

I went only _____ to the zoo.

STEP 9 You now know how to use once, which means "one time."

STEP 10 Write your own sentence using **once**.

_____

_____

_____

_____

WORD 63   **only**
(on) (ly)   **2 syllables**

Only means **"just,"** as used in the sentence:

I have **only** one very warm coat.

STEP 1   **Only** means "just " in:

I have **only** one very warm coat.

STEP 2   _____ means "just."

STEP 3   Softly say **only**, and clap once for each one of the two syllable sounds: **on** and **ly**

STEP 4   Write each syllable in **only**:

_____   _____

STEP 5   Circle or underline **only** in:

I have only one very warm coat.

STEP 6 "Just" means:

_____

STEP 7 Fill in the missing letters.

o ____ ____ y

STEP 8 Complete the sentence by using **only**, which means "just."

I have _____ one very warm coat.

STEP 9 You now know how to use **only**, which means "just."

STEP 10 Write your own sentence using **only**.

_____

_____

_____

_____

WORD 64 people
(peo) (ple) 2 syllables

People means "group of persons"

as used in the sentence:

About 100 **people** came to our school concert.

STEP 1 <u>People</u> means "group of persons" in:

About 100 **people** came to our school concert.

STEP 2 _____ means "group of persons."

STEP 3 Softly say **people**, and clap once for each one of the two syllable sounds: **peo** and **ple**

STEP 4 Write each syllable in **people**.

_____ _____

STEP 5 Circle or underline **people** in:

About 100 people came to our school concert.

STEP 6 "Group of persons" means:

_____

STEP 7 Fill in the missing letters.

p ____ ____ p ____ e

STEP 8 Complete the sentence by using **people**, which means "group of persons."

About 100 _____ came to our school concert.

STEP 9 You now know how to use **people**, which means "group of persons."

STEP 10 Write your own sentence using **people**.

_____

_____

_____

_____

WORD 65   perfect
(per) (fect) 2 syllables

Perfect means **"having nothing wrong,"**
as used in the sentence:

Jan had a **perfect** math test, with no mistakes.

STEP 1 **Perfect** means "having nothing wrong" in:
Jan had a **perfect** math test, with no mistakes.

STEP 2 _____ means "having nothing wrong."

STEP 3 Softly say **perfect**, and clap once for each one of the two syllable sounds: **per** and **fect**

STEP 4 Write each syllable in **perfect**.

_____ _____

STEP 5 Circle or underline **perfect** in:

Jan had a perfect math test, with no mistakes.

STEP 6 "Having nothing wrong" means:

_____

STEP 7 Fill in the missing letters.

p ____ ____ f ____ c t

STEP 8 Complete the sentence by using **perfect**, which means "having nothing wrong."

Jan had a _____ math test, with no mistakes.

STEP 9 You now know how to use **perfect** which means "having nothing wrong."

STEP 10 Write your own sentence using **perfect**.

_____

_____

_____

_____

WORD 66   piece
(piece) 1 syllable

Piece means "part of a whole,"

as used in the sentence:

There is one missing **piece** of the puzzle.

STEP 1 **Piece** means "part of a whole" in:

There is one missing **piece** of the puzzle.

STEP 2 _____ means "part of a whole."

STEP 3 Softly say **piece**, and clap once for the one syllable.

STEP 4 Write the one syllable word, **piece**.

_____

STEP 5 Circle or underline **piece** in:

There is one missing piece of the puzzle.

STEP 6 "Part of a whole " means:

_____

STEP 7 Fill in the missing letters.

p ____ ____ c e

STEP 8 Complete the sentence by using **piece** which means "part of a whole."

There is one missing _____ of the puzzle.

STEP 9 You now know how to use **piece**, which means "part of a whole."

STEP 10 Write your own sentence using **piece**.

_____

_____

_____

_____

> **WORD 67**   **question**
> (ques) (tion) 2 syllables
>
> **Question means "something asked,"**
>
> as used in the sentence:
>
> Ariel knew the answer to the **question**.

STEP 1   <u>Question</u> means "something asked" in:

Ariel knew the answer to the **question.**

STEP 2   _____ means "something asked."

STEP 3   Softly say **question**, and clap once for each one of the two syllable sounds: **ques** and **tion**

STEP 4   Write each syllable in **question**.

_____ _____

STEP 5   Circle or underline **question** in:

Ariel knew the answer to the question.

STEP 6 "Something asked" means:

_____

STEP 7 Fill in the missing letters.

q ___ ___ s ___ i o ___

STEP 8 Complete the sentence by using **question**, which means "something asked."

Ariel knew the answer to the _____.

STEP 9 You now know how to use **question**, which means "something asked."

STEP 10 Write your own sentence using **question**.

_____

_____

_____

_____

WORD 68   **said**
(said) 1 syllable

Said means **"spoke,"** as used in the sentence:

The weather reporter **said** it will rain today.

STEP 1 **Said** means "spoke" in:

The weather reporter **said** it will rain today.

STEP 2 _____ means "spoke."

STEP 3 Softly say **said**, and clap once for the one syllable.

STEP 4 Write the one syllable word, **said**.

_____

STEP 5 Circle or underline **said** in:

The weather reporter said it will rain today.

STEP 6 "Spoke " means:

_____

STEP 7 Fill in the missing letters.

s ____ ____ d

STEP 8 Complete the sentence by using **said**, which means "spoke."

The weather reporter _____ it will rain today.

STEP 9 You now know how to use **said**, which means "spoke."

STEP 10 Write your own sentence using **said**.

_____

_____

_____

_____

> **WORD 69** school
> (school) 1 syllable
>
> **School** means **"place for learning,"**
>
> as used in the sentence:
>
> My **school** has the best teachers.

STEP 1 <u>School</u> means "place for learning" in:

My **school** has the best teachers.

STEP 2 _____ means "place for learning."

STEP 3 Softly say **school**, and clap once for the one syllable.

STEP 4 Write the one syllable word, **school**.

_____

STEP 5 Circle or underline **school** in:

My school has the best teachers.

STEP 6 "Place for learning" means:

_____

STEP 7 Fill in the missing letters:

s ____ ____ o ____ l

STEP 8 Complete the sentence by using **school**, which means "place for learning."

My _____ has the best teachers.

STEP 9 You now know how to use **school**, which means "place for learning."

STEP 10 Write your own sentence using **school**.

_____

_____

_____

_____

WORD 70   **since**
(since) 1 syllable

Since means **"from that time until now,"** as used in the sentence:

I have been happy **since** I came to this school.

STEP 1 **Since** means "from that time until now" in:

I have been happy **since** I came to this school.

STEP 2 _____ means "from that time until now."

STEP 3 Softly say **since**, and clap once for the one syllable.

STEP 4 Write the one syllable word, **since**.

_____

STEP 5 Circle or underline **since** in:

I have been happy since I came to this school.

STEP 6 "From that time until now" means:

_____

STEP 7 Fill in the missing letters.

s ____ ____ c e

STEP 8 Complete the sentence by using **since**, which means "from that time until now.

I have been happy _____ I came to this school.

STEP 9 You now know how to use **since**, which means "from that time until now."

STEP 10 Write your own sentence using **since**.

_____

_____

_____

_____

WORD 71 **sister**
(sis) (ter) 2 syllables

Sister means **"girl with same mother or father,"**
as used in the sentence:

I have one **sister** and one brother who live at home.

STEP 1 **Sister** means "girl with same mother or father" in:

I have one **sister** and one brother who live at home.

STEP 2 _____ means "girl with same mother or father."

STEP 3 Softly say **sister**, and clap once for each one of the two syllable sounds: **sis** and **ter**

STEP 4 Write each syllable in **sister**.

_____   _____

STEP 5 Circle or underline **sister** in:

I have one sister and one brother who live at home.

STEP 6 "Girl with mother or father" means:

_____

STEP 7 Fill in the missing letters.

s ____ ____ t ____ r

STEP 8 Complete the sentence by using **sister**, which means "girl with same mother or father."

I have one _____ and brother who live at home.

STEP 9 You now know how to use **sister**, which means "girl with same mother or father."

STEP 10 Write your own sentence using **sister**.

_____

_____

_____

_____

> **WORD 72**   **sometimes**
> (some) (times) 2 syllables
>
> **Sometimes** means **"at times,"**
> as used in the sentence:
>
> **Sometimes** I wear my older sister's clothes.

STEP 1   **Sometimes** means "at times" in:

   Sometimes I wear my older sister's clothes.

STEP 2   _____ means "at times."

STEP 3   Softly say **sometimes**, and clap once for each one of the two syllable sounds: **some** and **times**

STEP 4   Write each syllable in **sometimes**.

   _____ _____

STEP 5   Circle or underline **sometimes** in:

   Sometimes I wear my older sister's clothes.

STEP 6 "At times" means:

_____

STEP 7 Fill in the missing letters.

s ____ ____ e ____ i ____ e s

STEP 8 Complete the sentence by using **sometimes**, which means "at times."

_____ I wear my older sister's clothes.

STEP 9 You now know how to use **sometimes**, which means "at times."

STEP 10 Write your own sentence using **sometimes**.

_____

_____

_____

_____

WORD 73 **sudden**
(sud) (den) 2 syllables

Sudden means **"happening fast,"**

as used in the sentence:

There was a **sudden** storm that flooded our street.

STEP 1 **Sudden** means "happening fast" in:

There was a **sudden** storm that flooded our street.

STEP 2 _____ means "happening fast."

STEP 3 Softly say **sudden**, and clap once for each one of the two syllable sounds: **sud** and **den**

STEP 4 Write each syllable in **sudden**.

_____ _____

STEP 5 Circle or underline **sudden** in:

There was a sudden storm that flooded our street.

STEP 6 "Happening fast" means:

_____

STEP 7 Fill in the missing letters.

s ____ ____ d ____ n

STEP 8 Complete the sentence by using **sudden**, which means "happening fast."

There was a _____ storm that flooded our street.

STEP 9 You now know how to use **sudden**, which means "happening fast."

STEP 10 Write your own sentence using **sudden**.

_____

_____

_____

_____

WORD 74   **that's**
(that's) 1 syllable

That's means **"that is,"** as used in the sentence:

This is my pencil, and **that's** yours.

STEP 1 **That's** means "that is" in:

This is my pencil, and **that's** yours.

STEP 2 _____ means "that is."

STEP 3 Softly say **that's**, and clap once for the one syllable.

STEP 4 Write the one syllable word, **that's**.

_____

STEP 5 Circle or underline **that's** in:

This is my pencil, and that's yours.

STEP 6 "That is" means:

_____

STEP 7 Fill in the missing letters.

t ____ ____ t ' ____

STEP 8 Complete the sentence by using **that's**, which means "that is.

This is my pencil, and _____ yours.

STEP 9 You now know how to use **that's** which means "that is."

STEP 10 Write your own sentence using **that's**.

_____

_____

_____

_____

WORD 75   **there**
(there) 1 syllable

There means **"at that place,"** as used in the sentence:

Please put the laptop over **there**.

STEP 1 **There** means "at that place" in:

Please put the laptop over **there**.

STEP 2 _____ means "at that place."

STEP 3 Softly say **there**, and clap once for the one syllable.

STEP 4 Write the one syllable word, **there**.

_____

STEP 5 Circle or underline **there** in:

Please put the laptop over there.

STEP 6 "At that place" means:

_____

STEP 7 Fill in the missing letters.

t ___ ___ r e

STEP 8 Complete the sentence by using **there**, which means "at that place."

Please put the laptop over_____.

STEP 9 You now know how to use **there**, which means "at that place."

STEP 10 Write your own sentence using **there**.

_____

_____

_____

WORD 76   **they**
(they) 1 syllable

They means **"more than one person"** in the sentence:

    They will have fun at the birthday party.

STEP 1 **They** means "more than one person" in:
    They will have fun at the birthday party.

STEP 2 _____ means "more than one person."

STEP 3 Softly say **they**, and clap once for the one syllable.

STEP 4 Write the one syllable word, **they**.

_____

STEP 5 Circle or underline **they** in:

    They will have fun at the birthday party.

STEP 6 "More than one person" means:

_____

STEP 7 Fill in the missing letters:

t ____ ____ y

STEP 8 Complete the sentence by using **they**, which means "more than one person."

_____ will have fun at the birthday party.

STEP 9 You now know how to use **they**, which means "more than one person."

STEP 10 Write your own sentence using **they**.

_____

_____

_____

_____

> **WORD 77** think
> (think) 1 syllable
>
> **Think** means **"have an idea,"**
> as used in the sentence:
>
> I **think** I will ride my bike today.

STEP 1 **Think** means "have an idea" in:

I **think** I will ride my bike today.

STEP 2 _____ means "have an idea."

STEP 3 Say **think**, and clap once for the one syllable.

STEP 4 Write the one syllable word, **think**.

_____

STEP 5 Circle or underline **think** in:

I think I will ride my bike today.

STEP 6 "Have an idea" means:

_____

STEP 7 Fill in the missing letters.

t ____ ____ n k

STEP 8 Complete the sentence by using **think**, which means "have an idea,"

I _____ I will ride my bike today.

STEP 9 You now know how to use **think**, which means "have an idea."

STEP 10 Write your own sentence using **think**.

_____

_____

_____

> **WORD 78** **this**
>
> (this) 1 syllable
>
> **This** means **"something close by,"**
>
> as used in the sentence:
>
> <u>This</u> pizza tastes so good.

STEP 1 <u>This</u> means "something close by" in:

<u>This</u> pizza tastes so good.

STEP 2 _____ means "something close by."

STEP 3 Softly say **this**, and clap once for the one syllable.

STEP 4 Write the one syllable word, **this**.

_____

STEP 5 Circle or underline **this** in:

This pizza tastes so good.

STEP 6 "Something close by" means:

_____

STEP 7 Fill in the missing letters.

t ____ ____ s

STEP 8 Complete the sentence by using **this**, which means "something close by."

_____ pizza tastes so good.

STEP 9 You now know how to use **this**, which means "something close by."

STEP 10 Write your own sentence using **this**.

_____

_____

_____

_____

WORD 79   **thought**
(thought) 1 syllable

Thought means **"had an idea,"** as used in the sentence:

Carla **thought** we should play chess after school.

STEP 1 **Thought** means "had an idea" in:
Carla **thought** we should play chess after school.

STEP 2 _____ means "had an idea."

STEP 3 Softly say **thought**, and clap once for the one syllable.

STEP 4 Write the one syllable word, **thought**.

_____

STEP 5 Circle or underline **thought** in:

Carla thought we should play chess after school.

STEP 6 "Had an idea" means:

_____

STEP 7 Fill in the missing letters.

t ____ ____ u g ____ t

STEP 8 Complete the sentence by using **thought**, which means "had an idea."

Carla _____ we should play chess after school.

STEP 9 You now know how to use **thought**, which means "had an idea."

STEP 10 Write your own sentence using **thought**.

_____

_____

_____

_____

WORD 80   **through**
(through) 1 syllable

"**Through**" means **"from one end and out,"**

as used in the sentence:

The large truck can go **through** the tunnel.

STEP 1 **Through** means "from one end and out" in:

The large truck can go **through** the tunnel.

STEP 2 _____ means "from one end and out."

STEP 3 Softly say **through**, and clap once for the one syllable.

STEP 4 Write the one syllable word, **through**.

_____

STEP 5 Circle or underline **through** in:

The large truck can go through the tunnel.

STEP 6 From one end and out" means:

_____

STEP 7 Fill in the missing letters.

t ____ r ____ u ____ h

STEP 8 Complete the sentence by using **through**, which means "from one end and out."

The large truck can go _____ the tunnel.

STEP 9 You now know how to use **through**, which means "from one end and out."

STEP 10 Write your own sentence using **through**.

_____

_____

_____

_____

> **WORD 81** **told**
>
> (told) 1 syllable
>
> **Told** means **"said something in words,"**
>
> as used in the sentence:
>
> My mother **told** a funny story.

STEP 1 **Told** means "said something in words" in:

My mother **told** a funny story.

STEP 2 _____ means "said something in words."

STEP 3 Softly say **told**, and clap once for the one syllable.

STEP 4 Write the one syllable word, **told**.

_____

STEP 5 Circle or underline **told** in:

My mother told a funny story.

STEP 6 "Said something in words" means:

_____

STEP 7 Fill in the missing letters for **told**.

t _____ l _____

STEP 8 Complete the sentence by using **told**, which means "said something in words."

My mother _____ a funny story.

STEP 9 Now you know how to use **told**, which means "said something in words."

STEP 10 Write your own sentence using **told**.

_____

_____

_____

WORD 82   **tree**

(tree) **1 syllable**

Tree means "plant with trunk and branches,"

as used in the sentence:

We liked eating the apples from our apple **tree**.

STEP 1 **Tree** means "plant with trunk and branches" in:

We liked eating the apples from our apple **tree**.

STEP 2 _____ means "plant with trunk and branches."

STEP 3 Softly say **tree**, and clap once for the one syllable.

STEP 4 Write the one syllable word, **tree**.

_____

STEP 5 Circle or underline **tree** in:

We liked eating the apples from our apple tree.

STEP 6 "Plant with trunk and branches" means:

_____

STEP 7 Fill in the missing letters for **tree**.

t _____ e _____

STEP 8 Complete the sentence by using **tree**, which means "plant with trunk and branches"

We liked eating the apples from our apple _____.

STEP 9 You now know how to use **tree**, which means "plant with trunk and branches."

STEP 10 Write your own sentence using **tree**.

_____

_____

_____

_____

WORD 83   **trip**
(trip) 1 syllable

Trip means **"travel plan to a place,"**

as used in the sentence:

They took a **trip** to the mountains.

STEP 1 **Trip** means "travel plan to a place" in:

They took a **trip** to the mountains.

STEP 2 _____ means "travel plan to a place."

STEP 3 Softly say **trip**, and clap once for the one syllable.

STEP 4 Write the one syllable word, **trip**.

_____

STEP 5 Circle or underline **trip** in:

They took a trip to the mountains.

STEP 6 "Travel plan to a place" means:

_____

STEP 7 Fill in the missing letters for **trip**.

t _____ i _____

STEP 8 Complete the sentence by using **trip**, which means "travel plan to a place."

They took a _____ to the mountains.

STEP 9 You now know how to use **trip**, which means "travel plan to a place."

STEP 10 Write your own sentence using **trip**.

_____

_____

_____

_____

> **WORD 84** truck
> (truck) 1 syllable
>
> **Truck** means **"large wheeled vehicle for carrying,"** as used in the sentence:
>
> We used a **truck** to move to our new home.

STEP 1 **Truck** means "large wheeled vehicle for carrying" in:

We used a **truck** to move to our new home.

STEP 2 _____ means "large wheeled vehicle for carrying."

STEP 3 Softly say **truck**, and clap once for the one syllable.

STEP 4 Write the one syllable word, **truck**.

_____

STEP 5 Circle or underline **truck** in:

We used a truck to move to our new home.

STEP 6 "Large wheeled vehicle for carrying" means:

_____

STEP 7 Fill in the missing letters for **truck**.

t _____ u _____ k

STEP 8 Complete the sentence by using **truck**, which means "large wheeled vehicle for carrying."

We used a _____ to move to our new home.

STEP 9 You now know how to use **truck** which means "large wheeled vehicle for carrying."

STEP 10 Write your own sentence using **truck**.

_____

_____

_____

_____

WORD 85 two
(two) 1 syllable

Two means **"the number 2,"** as used in the sentence:

It takes **two** people to dance the Tango.

STEP 1 **Two** means "the number 2" in:

It takes **two** people to dance the Tango.

STEP 2 _____ means "the number 2."

STEP 3 Softly say **two**, and clap once for the one syllable.

STEP 4 Write the one syllable word, **two**.

_____

STEP 5 Circle or underline **two in**:

It takes two people to dance the Tango.

STEP 6 "The number 2" means:

_____

STEP 7 Fill in the missing letter for **two**.

t _____ o

STEP 8 Complete the sentence by using **two** which means "the number 2."

It takes _____ people to dance the tango.

STEP 9 You now know how to use **two**, which means "the number 2."

STEP 10 Write your own sentence using **two**.

_____

_____

_____

_____

WORD 86   until
(un) (til) 2 syllables

Until means **"up to the time of,"** as used in the sentence:

We will play outside **until** dark.

STEP 1 **Until** means "up to the time of" in:

We will play outside **until** dark.

STEP 2 _____ means "up to the time of."

STEP 3 Softly say **until**, and clap once for each one of the two syllable sounds: **un** and **til**

STEP 4 Write each syllable in **until**.

_____ _____

STEP 5 Circle or underline **until** in:

We will play outside until dark.

STEP 6 "Up to the time of" means:

_____

STEP 7 Fill in the missing letters for **until**.

u _____ t i _____

STEP 8 Complete the sentence by using **until**, which means "up to the time of."

We will play outside _____ dark.

STEP 9 You now know how to use **until**, which means "up to the time of."

STEP 10 Write your own sentence using **until**.

_____

_____

_____

_____

WORD 87 use
(use) 1 syllable

Use means **"do something with,"**
as used in the sentence:

Pablo knew how to **use** a shovel to dig a hole.

STEP 1 **Use** means "do something with" in:

Pablo knew how to **use** a shovel to dig a hole.

STEP 2 _____ means "do something with."

STEP 3 Softly say **use**, and clap once for the one syllable.

STEP 4 Write the one syllable word, **use**.

_____

STEP 5 Circle or underline **use** in:

Pablo knew how to use a shovel to dig a hole.

STEP 6 "Do something with" means:

_____

STEP 7 Fill in the missing letter for **use**.

u _____ e

STEP 8 Complete the sentence by using **use**, which means "do something with."

Pablo knew how to _____ a shovel to dig a hole.

STEP 9 You now know how to use **use**, which means "do something with."

STEP 10 Write your own sentence using **use**.

_____

_____

_____

WORD 88   **usually**
(u) (su) (al) (ly) 4 syllables

Usually means **"most of the time,"**
as used in the sentence:

Chris **usually** walks to school.

STEP 1   **Usually** means "most of the time" in:

Chris **usually** walks to school.

STEP 2   _____ means "most of the time."

STEP 3   Softly say **usually**, and clap once for each one of the four syllable sounds: **u, su, al** and **ly**

STEP 4   Write each syllable in **usually**.

_____ _____ _____ _____

STEP 5   Circle or underline **usually** in:

Chris usually walks to school.

STEP 6 "Most of the time" means:

_____

STEP 7 Fill in the missing letters for **usually**.

u _____ u a _____ l y

STEP 8 Complete the sentence by using **usually**, which means "most of the time."

Chris _____ walks to school.

STEP 9 You now know how to use **usually**, which means "most of the time."

STEP 10 Write your own sentence using **usually**.

_____

_____

_____

_____

WORD 89   watch
(watch) 1 syllable

Watch means "look at carefully,"

as used in the sentence:

Lan and I like to **watch** the fireworks.

STEP 1 <u>Watch</u> means "look at carefully" in:

Lan and I like to **watch** the fireworks.

STEP 2 _____ means "look at carefully."

STEP 3 Softly say **watch**, and clap once for the one syllable.

STEP 4 Write the one syllable word, **watch**.

_____

STEP 5 Circle or underline **watch** in:

Lan and I like to watch the fireworks.

STEP 6 "Look at carefully" means:

_____

STEP 7 Fill in the missing letters for **watch**.

w _____ t c _____

STEP 8 Complete the sentence by using **watch**, which means "look at carefully."

Lan and I like to _____ the fireworks.

STEP 9 You now know how to use **watch**, which means "look at carefully."

STEP 10 Write your own sentence using **watch**.

_____

_____

_____

_____

WORD 90   **when**
(when) 1 syllable

When means **"at what time,"** as used in the sentence:

When does the show start?

STEP 1 **When** means "at what time" in:

When does the show start?

STEP 2 _____ means "at what time."

STEP 3 Softly say **when**, and clap once for the one syllable.

STEP 4 Write the one syllable word, **when**.

_____

STEP 5 Circle or underline **when** in:

When does the show start?

STEP 6 "At what time" means:

_____

STEP 7 Fill in the missing letters for **when**.

w _____ e _____

STEP 8 Complete the sentence by using **when**, which means "at what time.

_____ does the show start?

STEP 9 You now know how to use **when**, which means "at what time."

STEP 10 Write your own sentence using **when**.

_____

_____

_____

_____

WORD 91   **where**
(where) 1 syllable

Where means **"at what place,"** as used in the sentence:

I can't remember **where** I left my book.

STEP 1 **Where** means "at what place" in:

I can't remember **where** I left my book.

STEP 2 _____ means "at what place."

STEP 3 Softly say **where** and clap once for the one syllable.

STEP 4 Write the one syllable word, **where**.

_____

STEP 5 Circle or underline **where** in:

I can't remember where I left my book.

STEP 6 "At what place" means:

_____

STEP 7 Fill in the missing letters for **where**.

w _____ _____ r e

STEP 8 Complete the sentence by using **where**, which means "at what place."

I can't remember _____ I left my book.

STEP 9 You now know how to use **where**, which means "at what place."

STEP 10 Write your own sentence using **where**.

_____

_____

_____

_____

WORD 92   **which**
(which) 1 syllable

Which means **"what one,"** as used in the sentence:

Which of the books do you like best?

STEP 1 **Which** means "what one" in:

Which of the books do you like best?

STEP 2 _____ means "what one."

STEP 3 Softly say **which**, and clap once for the one syllable.

STEP 4 Write the one syllable word, **which**.

_____

STEP 5 Circle or underline **which** in:

Which of the books do you like best?

STEP 6 "What one" means:

_____

STEP 7 Fill in the missing letters for **which**.

w h _____ c _____

STEP 8 Complete the sentence by using **which**, which means "what one."

_____ of the books do you like best?

STEP 9 You now know how to use **which**, which means "what one."

STEP 10 Write your own sentence using **which**.

_____

_____

_____

_____

> **WORD 93**   **who**
> (who) 1 syllable
>
> **Who** means **"which one,"** as used in the sentence:
>
> **Who** wants to help the teacher after school?

STEP 1 **Who** means "which one" in:

     Who wants to help the teacher after school?

STEP 2 _____ means "which one."

STEP 3 Softly say **who**, and clap once for the one syllable.

STEP 4 Write the one syllable word, **who**.

     _____

STEP 5 Circle or underline **who** in:

     Who wants to help the teacher after school?

STEP 6 "Which one" means:

_____

STEP 7 Fill in the missing letter for **who**.

w _____ o

STEP 8 Complete the sentence by using **who**, which means "which one."

_____ wants to help the teacher after school?

STEP 9 You now know how to use **who**, which means "which one."

STEP 10 Write your own sentence using **who**.

_____

_____

_____

WORD 94   **whole**
(whole) 1 syllable

Whole means **"total,"** as used in the sentence:

I felt that I could eat the **whole** pizza.

STEP 1 **Whole** means "total" in:

I felt that I could eat the **whole** pizza.

STEP 2 _____ means "total."

STEP 3 Softly say **whole**, and clap once for the one syllable.

STEP 4 Write the one syllable word, **whole**.

_____

STEP 5 Circle or underline **whole** in:

I felt that I could eat the whole pizza.

STEP 6 "Total" means:

_____

STEP 7 Fill in the missing letters for **whole**.

w _____ o _____ e

STEP 8 Complete the sentence by using **whole**, which means "total."

I felt that I could eat the _____ pizza.

STEP 9 You now know how to use **whole**, which mean "total."

STEP 10 Write your own sentence using **whole**.

_____

_____

_____

_____

WORD 95 **winner**
(win) (ner) 2 syllables

Winner means **"best in a contest,"** as used in the sentence:

Maria was the **winner** of the spelling bee.

STEP 1 **Winner** means "best in a contest" in:

Maria was the **winner** of the spelling bee.

STEP 2 _____ means "**winner.**"

STEP 3 Softly say **winner**, and clap once for each one of the two syllable sounds: **win** and **ner**

STEP 4 Write each syllable in **winner**.

_____ _____

STEP 5 Circle or underline **winner** in:

Maria was the winner of the spelling bee.

STEP 6 "Best in a contest" means:

_____

STEP 7 Fill in the missing letters for **winner**.

w _____ n _____ e r

STEP 8 Complete the sentence by using **winner**, which means "best in a contest."

Maria was the _____ of the spelling bee.

STEP 9 You now know how to use **winner**, which means "best in a contest."

STEP 10 Write your own sentence using **winner**.

_____

_____

_____

_____

WORD 96 won't
(won't) 1 syllable

Won't means **"will not,"** as used in the sentence:

The copy machine **won't** print good copies.

STEP 1 **Won't** means "will not" in:

   The copy machine **won't** print good copies.

STEP 2 _____ means "will not."

STEP 3 Softly say **won't**, and clap once for the one syllable.

STEP 4 Write the one syllable word, **won't**.

   _____

STEP 5 Circle or underline **won't** in:

   The copy machine won't print good copies.

STEP 6 "Will not" means:

_____

STEP 7 Fill in the missing letters for **won't**.

w _____ n ' _____

STEP 8 Complete the sentence by using **won't**, which means "will not."

The copy machine _____ print good copies.

STEP 9 You now know how to use **won't** which means "will not."

STEP 10 Write your own sentence using **won't**.

_____

_____

_____

_____

WORD 97 wouldn't
(would) (n't) 2 syllables

Wouldn't means **"would not,"** as used in the sentence:

Wouldn't you like to go to the parade?

STEP 1 **Wouldn't** means "boy with same parents" in:

Wouldn't you like to go to the parade?

STEP 2 _____ means "would not."

STEP 3 Softly say **wouldn't**, and clap once for each one of the two syllable sounds: **would** and **n't**

STEP 4 Write each syllable in **wouldn't**.

_____ _____

STEP 5 Circle or underline **wouldn't** in:

Wouldn't you like to go to the parade?

STEP 6 "Would not" means:

_____

STEP 7 Fill in the missing letters for **wouldn't**..

w _____ u l _____n ' _____

STEP 8 Complete the sentence by using **wouldn't**, which means "would not."

_____ you like to go to the parade?

STEP 9 You now know how to use **wouldn't**, which means "would not."

STEP 10 Write your own sentence using **wouldn't**.

_____

_____

_____

_____

WORD 98   **write**
(write) 1 syllable

"Write" means "form words," as used in the sentence:

You may **write** with a pen, crayon or chalk.

STEP 1 **Write** means "form words" in:

You may **write** with a pen, crayon or chalk.

STEP 2 _____ means "form words."

STEP 3 Softly say **write**, and clap once for the one syllable.

STEP 4 Write the one syllable word, **write**.

_____

STEP 5 Circle or underline **write** in:

You may write with a pen, crayon or chalk.

STEP 6 "Form words" means:

_____

STEP 7 Fill in the missing letters for **write**.

w _____ i _____ e

STEP 8 Complete the sentence by using **write** which means "form words."

You may _____ with a pen, crayon or chalk.

STEP 9 You now know how to use **write**, which means "form words."

STEP 10 Write your own sentence using **write**.

_____

_____

_____

WORD 99   **year**
(year) 1 syllable

Year means **"12 months,"** as used in the sentence:

Birthdays come every year.

STEP 1 <u>Year</u> means "12 months" in:

Birthdays come every **year**.

STEP 2 _____ means "12 months."

STEP 3 Softly say **year**, and clap once for the one syllable.

STEP 4 Write the one syllable word, **year**.

_____

STEP 5 Circle or underline **year** in:

Birthdays come every year.

STEP 6 "12 months" means:

_____

STEP 7 Fill in the missing letters for **year**.

y _____ a r

STEP 8 Complete the sentence by using **year**, which means "12 months."

Birthdays come every _____.

STEP 9 You now know how to use **year**, which means "12 months."

STEP 10 Write your own sentence using **year**.

_____

_____

_____

_____

WORD 100 young
(young) 1 syllable

Young means **"not old,"** as used in the sentence:

Puppies are **young** dogs.

STEP 1 <u>Young</u> means "not old" in:

Puppies are **young** dogs.

STEP 2 _____ means "not old."

STEP 3 Softly say **young**, and clap once for the one syllable.

STEP 4 Write the one syllable word, **young**.

_____

STEP 5 Circle or underline **young** in:

Puppies are young dogs.

STEP 6 "Not old" means:

_____

STEP 7 Fill in the missing letters for **young**.

y _____ u _____ g

STEP 8 Complete the sentence by using **young**, which means "not old."

Puppies are _____ dogs.

STEP 9 You now know how to use **young**, which means "not old."

STEP 10 Write your own sentence using **young**.

_____

_____

_____

_____

2. TESTS

DIRECTIONS

HOW TO TEST MY WORD LEARNING

1. Take a test for each Word Group of 10 words after studying each Word Group.

2. Choose the correct meaning for the 10 words on each test.

3. Check the page numbers for each of the tests next on page 215.

TESTS
WORD GROUPS 1 – 10

Group 1 (Words 1-10)…........page 216

Group 2 (Words 11-20)........page 218

Group 3 (Words 21-30)........page 220

Group 4 (Words 31-40).......page 222

Group 5 (Words 41-50)…....page 224

Group 6 (Words 51-60)........page 226

Group 7 (Words 61-70)…....page 228

Group 8 (Words 71-80)…....page 230

Group 9 (Words 81-90)........page 232

Group 10 (Words 91-100)....page 234

WORD GROUP 1 TEST: Words 1-10

Choose the correct meaning for the underlined word.

1. We have <u>about</u> an hour until lunch.

    a. almost

    b. ever

    c. surely

    d. happily

2. My cousin will come <u>again</u> to visit soon.

    a. never

    b. another time

    c. inside

    d. nicely

3. Remember <u>always</u> to brush your teeth daily.

    a. every time

    b. sometimes

    c. two

    d. never

4. I would like <u>another</u> piece of pizza.

    a. one more

    b. no other

    c. a small

    d. a large

5. Has <u>anyone</u> found my backpack?

    a. everyone

    b. someone not named

    c. my friend

    d. all

6. Keisha **asked** a friend to visit after school.

    a. phoned   c. told

    b. questioned   d. believed

7. We saw a **beautiful** sunset.

    a. cold   c. good-looking

    b. dark   d. lighted

8. We will be home **before** dark.

    a. wanting   c. instead of

    b. ahead of   d. after

9. My parents could not **believe** that they won a car.

    a. think it is true   c. help

    b. like   d. be sad

10. Try to do your **best** work.

    a. finest   c. last

    b. fastest   d. kindest

WORD GROUP 2 TEST: Words 11-20

Choose the correct meaning for the underlined word.

11. My sister and I <u>both</u> have games today.

   a. do
   b. one and another
   c. don't
   d. decided to

12. Lee has one <u>brother</u> and one sister.

   a. twin
   b. relative
   c. boy with same mother or father
   d. family

13. Azra is going to <u>build</u> a large cage for the rabbit.

   a. draw
   b. make something
   c. buy up
   d. take

14. My mother is very <u>busy</u> at the computer.

   a. active
   b. happy
   c. lazy
   d. tired

15. Money can't <u>buy</u> happiness.

   a. cure
   b. pay a price for
   c. hold
   d. thank

16. I will carry the groceries home from the store.

    a. phone   c. hold while moving

    b. follow   d. keep track of

17. I ran and caught the ball.

    a. got something moving   c. missed

    b. hit   d. threw

18. Ten children play in the school band.

    a. young people   c. kinds

    b. families   d. cousins

19. A city has more people than a town.

    a. mall   c. farm houses

    b. where many people live   d. hallway

20. I didn't know Nan could play the drums.

    a. should   c. would

    b. might   d. was able to

WORD GROUP 3 TEST: Words 21-30

Choose the correct meaning for the underlined word.

21. The mouse from the <u>country</u> does not like the city.

    a. city land   c. land outside cities and towns

    b. gray   d. tree

22. I have one <u>cousin</u> whose mother is my Aunt Ann.

    a. group member   c. child of aunt or uncle

    b. relative   d. friend

23. "<u>Dear</u> Dan," began the letter.

    a. loved   c. absent

    b. not liked   d. happy

24. Jake <u>didn't</u> knock before going into the house.

    a. did so   c. does

    b. did not   d. does not

25. Dogs and cats are <u>different</u>.

    a. very easy   c. not the same

    b. good as   d. the same as

26. Our class <u>does</u> good work.

    a. performs   c. likes

    b. wants   d. can't do

27. My friend <u>doesn't</u> want to go shopping today.

    a. wouldn't   c. has not

    b. does not   d. can not

28. Have you <u>done</u> your homework?

    a. finished   c. tried

    b. missed   d. stopped

29. A locked <u>door</u> opens with a key.

    a. plate   c. hat

    b. drink   d. something that closes off space

30. My baby sister will <u>drink</u> all of the milk.

    a. swallow liquid   c. want

    b. dislike   d. push away

WORD GROUP 4 TEST: Words 31-40

Circle the correct meaning for the underlined word.

31. I don't want to <u>drop</u> my ice cream cone.

    a. try

    b. cover

    c. not eat

    d. let fall

32. It is <u>easy</u> to read with my new glasses.

    a. careless

    b. not hard to do

    c. bad

    d. not good

33. We have <u>enough</u> food for the party.

    a. not

    b. as much as needed

    c. a little

    d. less

34. <u>Every</u> student went on the class trip.

    a. all in a group

    b. none

    c. one

    d. no

35. I can close one <u>eye</u> at a time.

    a. room

    b. hat

    c. body part for seeing

    d. foot

36. My nose and eyes are on my face.

    a. front part of the head   c. foot

    b. part of arm   d. neck

37. A is the first letter of the alphabet.

    a. best   c. third

    b. before all else   d. last

38. Our food market has over forty ice cream flavors.

    a. the number 40   c. five

    b. the number 41   d. four plus zero

39. I met the new girl in class.

    a. sister   c. female child

    b. mother   d. grown-up

40. I would like to give you a special present.

    a. let have   c. read

    b. never have   d. hide

WORD GROUP 5 TEST: Words 41-50

Choose the correct meaning for the underlined word.

41. My apple tastes <u>good</u>.

    a. very cold   c. warm

    b. soft   d. very fine

42. I had a <u>great</u> time at my new school today.

    a. bright   c. silly

    b. very good   d. bad

43. We want our team to <u>have</u> new shirts.

    a. own   c. walk

    b. like   d. owe

44 The eyes, ears, nose and mouth are all part of the <u>head</u>.

    a. shoes   c. body part above the neck

    b. neck   d. knees

45. I <u>heard</u> the thunder before the storm.

    a. found   c. stopped

    b. listened to   d. liked

46. My cat, Fluff, is <u>here</u> in the kitchen.

    a. where you are now   c. happy

    b. away   d. asleep

47. We have two families living in our <u>house</u>.

    a. cave   c. building where people live

    b. tent   d. room

48. The flu shot did not <u>hurt</u>.

    a. have a feeling of pain   c. fall

    b. last long   d. work

49. What a good <u>idea</u> to take an umbrella on this rainy day!

    a. event   c. find

    b. time   d. thought

50. <u>It's</u> a good day in the neighborhood.

    a. it is   c. it is not

    b. its   d. it will be

WORD GROUP 6 TEST: Words 51-60

Choose the correct meaning for the underlined word.

51. I knew all the answers on the test.

   a. never had
   c. loved
   b. was sure of
   d. wanted

52. Whales are large animals.

   a. walking
   c. small
   b. very young
   d. big

53. Barbara turned on the light to read the book.

   a. heat for warming
   c. lock
   b. lamp for seeing
   d. TV

54. Janna loves to listen to music.

   a. make sounds
   c. talk
   b. hear carefully
   d. dance

55. Look at the beautiful sunset.

   a. use eyes to see
   c. sing
   b. smile
   d. great

56. I got the mail in our mailbox.

    a. sent, as by the post office   c. what goes into the trash

    b. games   d. shirts

57. Manny will make dinner tonight.

    a. put together   c. run to

    b. tell about   d. see

58. Many people have cell phones.

    a. a large number of   c. a few

    b. watch   d. two

59. Hanna helped me measure the room.

    a. make up   c. take out

    b. find out the size of   d. build

60. We have more than 20 pens.

    a. lower   c. other

    b. less   d. a larger number

WORD GROUP 7 TEST: Words 61-70

Choose the correct meaning for the underlined word.

61. We go to the park <u>often</u> in the summer.

    a. sometimes   c. never

    b. many times   d. happily

62. I went only <u>once</u> to the zoo.

    a. never   c. two times

    b. outside   d. one time

63. I have <u>only</u> one very warm coat.

    a. many   c. more than

    b. just   d. not

64. About 100 <u>people</u> came to our school concert.

    a. group of persons   c. words

    b. nobody   d. cats

65. Jen had a <u>perfect</u> math test, with no mistakes.

    a. having nothing wrong   c. only

    b. bad   d. surprise

66. There is one missing <u>piece</u> of the puzzle.

    a. part of a whole   c. sheep

    b. group in the room   d. person

67. Ariel knew the answer to the <u>question</u>.

    a. something asked   c. plan

    b. words   d. name

68. The weather reporter <u>said</u> it will rain today.

    a. spoke   c. meant

    b. cried   d. after

69. My <u>school</u> has the best teachers.

    a. every place   c. place for learning

    b. buildings   d. street light

70. I have been happy <u>since</u> I came to this school.

    a. from that time until now   c. working hard

    b. before that time   d. never

WORD GROUP 8 TEST: Words 71-80

Choose the correct meaning for the underlined word.

71. I have one <u>sister</u> and one brother who live at home.

    a. family

    b. cousin

    c. friend with no brothers

    d. girl with same mother or father

72. <u>Sometimes</u> I wear my older sister's clothes.

    a. surely

    b. at times

    c. never before

    d. always

73. There was a <u>sudden</u> storm that flooded our street.

    a. not happening

    b. loud

    c. happening fast

    d. thunder

74. This is my pencil, and <u>that's</u> yours.

    a. this was

    b. that is

    c. it has

    d. that does

75. Please put the laptop over <u>there</u>.

    a. my game

    b. at that place

    c. for the best

    d. food

76. <u>They</u> will have fun at the birthday party.

    a. one person

    b. more than one person

    c. ball games

    d. nobody

77. I <u>think</u> I will ride my bike today.

    a. said

    b. have a pain

    c. dance

    d. have an idea

78. <u>This</u> pizza tastes so good.

    a. eating

    b. all

    c. something close by

    d. far away

79. Carla <u>thought</u> we should play chess after school.

    a. had an idea

    b. was tired

    c. came

    d. had something

80. The large truck can go <u>through</u> the tunnel.

    a. ever

    b. on the water

    c. from one end and out

    d. over

WORD GROUP 9 TEST: Words 81-90

Choose the correct meaning for the underlined word.

81. My mother <u>told</u> a story about her childhood.

    a. thought   c. said something in words

    b. took a trip   d. sang a song

82. We liked eating the apples from our apple <u>tree</u>.

    a. small flowers   c. rose bushes

    b. lawn   d. plant with trunk and branches

83. They took a <u>trip</u> to the mountains.

    a. house   c. different place

    b. school   d. travel plan to a place

84. We used a <u>truck</u> to move to our new home.

    a. small car with wheels   c. large wheeled vehicle for carrying

    b. large boat   d. large car with wings

85. It takes <u>two</u> people to dance the tango.

    a. no   c. any number

    b. the number 2   d. all

86. We will play outside <u>until</u> dark.

    a. up to the time of   c. always

    b. for all   d. only

87. He knew how to <u>use</u> a shovel to dig a hole

    a. do with something   c. buy

    b. very good way   d. make

88. Chris <u>usually</u> walks to school.

    a. never   c. does not

    b. most of the time   d. only once

89. Lan and I like to <u>watch</u> the fireworks.

    a. take out   c. make carefully

    b. look at carefully   d. use

90. <u>When</u> does the show start?

    a. at what time   c. the first time

    b. until   d. here

WORD GROUP 10 TEST: Words 91-100

Choose the correct meaning for the underlined word

91. I can't remember <u>where</u> I left my book.

    a. through   c. when

    b. in that time   d. at what place

92. <u>Which</u> of the books do you like best?

    a. look at   c. what one

    b. where   d. when

93. <u>Who</u> wants to help the teacher after school?

    a. which one   c. when

    b. where one   d. how

94. I felt I could eat the <u>whole</u> pizza.

    a. good   c. real

    b. best   d. total

95. Maria was the <u>winner</u> of the spelling bee.

    a. cook   c. friend in a game

    b. not good   d. best in a contest

96. The copy machine won't print good copies..

    a. weren't   c. will not

    b. is not   d. wanted

97. Wouldn't you like to go to the parade?

    a. would not   c. didn't

    b. does not   d. have not

98. You may write with a pen, crayon or chalk.

    a. form words   c. listen

    b. talk   d. dream

99. Birthdays come every year.

    a. week   c. 12 months

    b. month   d. day

100. Puppies are young dogs.

    a. helping   c. not old

    b. best   d. old

3. TESTS ANSWER KEYS

DIRECTIONS

HOW TO FIND OUT WHAT I LEARNED

1. Compare your test answers with the answers on the Tests Answer Keys.

2. Mark each correct answer on your tests.

3. Check the page numbers for the Test Answer Keys next on page 237.

TESTS ANSWER KEYS
WORD GROUPS 1 – 10

Group 1 (Words 1-10)……....page 238

Group 2 (Words 11-20)........page 240

Group 3 (Words 21-30)........page 242

Group 4 (Words 31-40)........page 244

Group 5 (Words 41-50)…....page 246

Group 6 (Words 51-60)........page 248

Group 7 (Words 61-70)…....page 250

Group 8 (Words 71-80)…....page 252

Group 9 (Words 81-90)........page 254

Group 10 (Words 91-100)....page 256

WORD GROUP 1 TEST ANSWER KEYS: Words 1-10

Check your test answers with the correct words below.

1. We have <u>about</u> an hour until lunch.

    a. <u>almost</u>   c. surely

    b. ever   d. happily

2. My cousin will come <u>again</u> to visit soon.

    a. never   c. inside

    b. <u>another time</u>   d. nicely

3. Remember <u>always</u> to brush your teeth daily.

    a. <u>every time</u>   c. two

    b. sometimes   d. sometimes

4. I would like <u>another</u> piece of pizza.

    a. <u>one more</u>   c. a small

    b. no other   d. a large

5. Has <u>anyone</u> found my backpack?

    a. everyone   c. Max

    b. <u>someone not named</u>   d. all

238

6. Keisha **asked** a friend to visit after school.

   a. phoned

   b. questioned

   c. told

   d. believed

7. We saw a **beautiful** sunset.

   a. cold

   b. dark

   c. good-looking

   d. lighted

8. We will be home **before** dark.

   a. wanting

   b. ahead of

   c. instead of

   d. after

9. My parents could not **believe** that they won a car.

   a. think it is true

   b. like

   c. help

   d. be sad

10. Try to do your **best** work.

    a. finest

    b. fastest

    c. last

    d. kindest

WORD GROUP 2 TEST ANSWER KEYS: Words 11-20

Check your test answers with the correct words below.

11. My sister and I <u>both</u> have games today.

    a. do

    b. <u>one and another</u>

    c. don't

    d. decided to

12. Lee has one <u>brother</u> and one sister.

    a. twin

    b. relative

    c. <u>boy with same mother or father</u>

    d. family

13. Azra is going to <u>build</u> a large cage for the rabbit.

    a. draw

    b. <u>make something</u>

    c. buy up

    d. take

14. My mother is very <u>busy</u> at the computer.

    a. <u>active</u>

    b. happy

    c. lazy

    d. tired

15. Money can't <u>buy</u> happiness.

    a. cure

    b. <u>pay a price for</u>

    c. hold

    d. thank

16. I will <u>carry</u> the groceries home from the store.

    a. phone

    b. follow

    c. <u>hold while moving</u>

    d. keep track of

17. I ran and <u>caught</u> the ball.

    a. <u>got something moving</u>

    b. hit

    c. missed

    d. threw

18. Ten <u>children</u> play in the school band.

    a. <u>young people</u>

    b. families

    c. kinds

    d. cousins

19. A <u>city</u> has more people than a town.

    a. mall

    b. <u>where many people live</u>

    c. farm houses

    d. hallway

20. I didn't know Nan <u>could</u> play the drums.

    a. should

    b. might

    c. would

    d. <u>was able to</u>

WORD GROUP 3 TEST ANSWER KEYS: Words 21-30

Check your test answers with the correct words below.

21. The mouse from the <u>country</u> does not like the city.

    a. city land   c. <u>land outside cities and towns</u>

    b. gray   d. tree

22. I have one <u>cousin</u> whose mother is my Aunt Ann.

    a. group member   c. <u>child of aunt or uncle</u>

    b. relative   d. friend

23. "<u>Dear</u> Dan," began the letter.

    a. <u>loved</u>   c. absent

    b. not liked   d. happy

24. Jake <u>didn't</u> knock before going into the house.

    a. did so   c. does

    b. <u>did not</u>   d. does not

25. Dogs and cats are <u>different</u>.

    a. very easy   c. <u>not the same</u>

    b, bad as   d. the same as

26. Our class does good work.

    a. performs   c. likes

    b. wants   d. can't do

27. My friend doesn't want to go shopping today.

    a. wouldn't   c. has not

    b. does not   d. lighted

28. Have you done your homework?

    a. finished   c. tried

    b. missed   d. stopped

29. A locked door opens with a key.

    a. plate   c. hat

    b. drink   d. something that closes off space

30. My baby sister will drink all of the milk.

    a. swallow liquid   c. want

    b. dislike   d. push away

WORD GROUP 4 TEST ANSWER KEYS: Words 31-40

Check your test answers with the correct words below.

31. I don't want to drop my ice cream cone.

   a. try   c. not eat

   b. cover   d. let fall

32. It is easy to read with my new glasses.

   a. careless   c. bad

   b. not hard to do   d. not good

33. We have enough food for the party.

   a. not   c. a little

   b. as much as needed d. less

34. Every student went on the class trip.

   a. all in a group   c. one

   b. none   d. no

35. I can close one eye at a time..

   a. room   c. body part for seeing

   b. hat   d. foot

244

36. My nose and eyes are on my face.

   a. front part of the head
   c. foot
   b. part of arm
   d. neck

37. A is the first letter of the alphabet.

   a. best
   c. third
   b. before all else
   d. last

38. Our food market has over forty ice cream flavors.

   a. the number 40
   c. five
   b. the number 41
   d. four plus zero

39. I met the new girl in class.

   a. sister
   c. female child
   b. mother
   d. grown-up

40. I would like to give you a special present.

   a. let have
   c. read
   b. never have
   d. hide

WORD GROUP 5 TEST ANSWER KEYS: Words 41-50

Check your test answers with the correct words below.

41. My apple tastes <u>good</u>.

    a. very cold   c. warm

    b. soft   d. <u>very fine</u>

42. I had a <u>great</u> time at my new school today.

    a. bright   c. silly

    b. <u>very good</u>   d. bad

43. We want our team to <u>have</u> new shirts.

    a. <u>own</u>   c. walk

    b. like   d. owe

44. The eyes, ears, nose and mouth are all part of the <u>head</u>.

    a. shoes   c. <u>body part above the neck</u>

    b. neck   d. knees

45. I <u>heard</u> the thunder before the storm.

    a. found   c. stopped

    b. <u>listened to</u>   d. liked

46. My cat, Fluff, is <u>here</u> in the kitchen.

    a. <u>where you are now</u>   c. happy

    b. away   d. asleep

47. We have two families living in our <u>house</u>.

    a. cave   c. <u>building where people live</u>

    b. tent   d. room

48. The flu shot did not <u>hurt</u>.

    a. <u>have a feeling of pain</u>   c. fall

    b. last long   d. work

49. What a good <u>idea</u> to take an umbrella on this rainy day!

    a. event   c. find

    b. time   d. <u>thought</u>

50. <u>It's</u> a good day in the neighborhood.

    a. <u>it is</u>   c. it is not

    b. its   d. it will be

WORD GROUP 6 TEST ANSWER KEYS: Words 51-60

Check your test answers with the correct words below.

51. I <u>knew</u> all the answers on the test.

    a. never had   c. loved

    b. <u>was sure of</u>   d. wanted

52. Whales are <u>large</u> animals.

    a. walking   c. small

    b. very young   d. <u>big</u>

53. Barbara turned on the <u>light</u> to read the book.

    a. heat for warming   c. lock

    b. <u>lamp for seeing</u>   d. TV

54. Janna loves to <u>listen</u> to music.

    a. make sounds   c. talk

    b. <u>hear carefully</u>   d. dance

55. <u>Look</u> at the beautiful sunset.

    a. <u>use eyes to see</u>   c. sing

    b. smile   d. great

56. I got the <u>mail</u> in our mailbox.

    a. <u>sent, as by the post office</u>   c. what goes into the trash

    b. games   d. shirts

57. Manny will <u>make</u> dinner tonight.

    a. <u>put together</u>   c. run to

    b. tell about   d. see

58. <u>Many</u> people have cell phones.

    a. <u>a large number of</u>   c. a few

    b. watch   d. two

59. Hanna helped me <u>measure</u> the room.

    a. make up   c. take out

    b. <u>find out the size of</u>   d. build

60. We have <u>more</u> than 20 pens.

    a. lower   c. other

    b. less   d. <u>a larger number</u>

WORD GROUP 7 TEST ANSWER KEYS: Words 61-70

Check your test answers with the correct words below.

61. We go to the park <u>often</u> in the summer.

    a. sometimes   c. never

    b. <u>many times</u>   d. happily

62. I went only <u>once</u> to the zoo.

    a. never   c. two times

    b. outside   d. <u>one time</u>

63. I have <u>only</u> one very warm coat.

    a. many   c. more than

    b. <u>just</u>   d. not

64. About 100 <u>people</u> came to our school concert.

    a. <u>group of persons</u>   c. words

    b. nobody   d. cats

65. Jen had a <u>perfect</u> math test, with no mistakes.

    a. <u>having nothing wrong</u>   c. only

    b. bad   d. surprise

66. There is one missing <u>piece</u> of the puzzle.

    a. <u>part of a whole</u>   c. sheep

    b. group in the room   d. person

67. Ariel knew the answer to the <u>question</u>.

    a. <u>something asked</u>   c. plan

    b. words   d. name

68. The weather reporter <u>said</u> it will rain today.

    a. <u>spoke</u>   c. meant

    b. cried   d. after

69. My <u>school</u> has the best teachers.

    a. every place   c. <u>place for learning</u>

    b. buildings   d. street light

70. I have been happy <u>since</u> I came to this school.

    a. <u>from that time until now</u>   c. working hard

    b. before that time   d. never

WORD GROUP 8 TEST ANSWER KEYS: Words 71-80

Check your test answers with the correct words below.

71. I have one <u>sister</u> and one brother who live at home.

    a. family   c. friend with no brothers

    b. cousin   d. <u>girl with same mother or father</u>

72. <u>Sometimes</u> I wear my older sister's clothes.

    a. surely   c. never before

    b. <u>at times</u>   d. always

73. There was a <u>sudden</u> storm that flooded our street.

    a. not happening   c. <u>happening fast</u>

    b. loud   d. thunder

74. This is my pencil, and <u>that's</u> yours.

    a. this was   c. it has

    b. <u>that is</u>   d. that does

75. Please put the laptop over <u>there</u>.

    a. my game   c. for the best

    b. <u>at that place</u>   d. food

76. <u>They</u> will have fun at the birthday party.

   a. one person   c. ball games

   b. <u>more than one person</u>   d. nobody

77. I <u>think</u> I will ride my bike today.

   a. said   c. dance

   b. have a pain   d. <u>have an idea</u>

78. <u>This</u> pizza tastes so good.

   a. eating   c. <u>something close by</u>

   b. all   d. a person far away

79. Carla <u>thought</u> we should play chess after school.

   a. <u>had an idea</u>   c. came

   b. was tired   d. had something

80. The large truck can go <u>through</u> the tunnel?

   a. ever   c. <u>from one end and out</u>

   b on the water   d. over

253

WORD GROUP 9 TEST ANSWER KEYS: Words 81-90

Check your test answers with the correct words below.

81. My mother <u>told</u> a funny story.

   a. thought
   b. took a trip
   c. <u>said something in words</u>
   d. sang a song

82. We liked eating the apples from our apple <u>tree</u>.

   a. small flowers
   b. lawn
   c. rose bushes
   d. <u>plant with trunk and branches</u>

83. They took a <u>trip</u> to the mountains.

   a. house
   b. school
   c. different place
   d. <u>travel plan to a place</u>

84. We used a <u>truck</u> to move to our new home.

   a. small car with wheels
   b. large boat
   c. <u>large wheeled vehicle for carrying</u>
   d. large car with wings

85. It takes <u>two</u> people to dance the tango.

   a. no
   b. <u>the number 2</u>
   c. any number
   d. all

86. We will play outside <u>until</u> dark.

    a. <u>up to the time of</u>   c. always

    b. for all   d. only

87. Pablo knew how to <u>use</u> a shovel to dig a hole.

    a. <u>do something with</u>   c. buy

    b. very good way   d. make

88. Chris <u>usually</u> walks to school.

    a. never   c. does not

    b. <u>most of the time</u>   d. only once

89. Lan and I like to <u>watch</u> the fireworks.

    a. take out   c. make carefully

    b. <u>look at carefully</u>   d. use

90. <u>When</u> does the show start?

    a. <u>at what time</u>   c. the first time

    b. until   d. here

WORD GROUP 10 TEST ANSWER KEYS: Words 91-100

Check your test answers with the correct words below.

91. I can't remember <u>where</u> I left my book.

    a. through   c. when

    b. in that time   d. <u>at what place</u>

92. <u>Which</u> of the books do you like best?

    a. look at   c. <u>what one</u>

    b. where   d. when

93. <u>Who</u> wants to help the teacher after school?

    a. <u>which one</u>   c. when

    b. where one   d. how

94. I felt I could eat the <u>whole</u> pizza.

    a. good   c. real

    b. best   d. <u>total</u>

95. Maria was the <u>winner</u> of the spelling bee.

    a. cook   c. friend in a game

    b. not good   d. <u>best in a contest</u>

96. The copy machine won't print good copies.

    a. weren't   c. will not

    b. is not   d. wanted

97. Wouldn't you like to go to the parade?

    a. would not   c. didn't

    b. does not   d. have not

98. You may write with a pen, crayon or chalk.

    a. form words   c. listen

    b. talk   d. dream

99. Birthdays come every year.

    a. week   c. 12 months

    b. month   d. day

100. Puppies are young dogs.

    a. helping   c. not old

    b. best   d. old

4. CHECKLISTS OF LEARNED WORDS

DIRECTIONS

HOW TO USE MY CHECKLISTS

1. After correcting your tests, you will fill out "My Checklists of Learned Words" on the next pages.

2. Mark each one of your learned words on the Word Group checklists.

3. Review words, if needed, and re-take tests until you have learned all 100 words.

3. Check the page numbers below for each of the Word Group checklists.

Word Groups 1 and 2…..page 260

Word Groups 3 and 4…..page 261

Word Groups 5 and 6…..page 262

Word Groups 7 and 8…..page 263

Word Groups 9 and 10…page 264

CHECKLISTS OF LEARNED WORDS

Word Groups 1 and 2

Word Group 1

___1. about

___2. again

___3. always

___4. another

___5. anyone

___6. asked

___7. beautiful

___8. before

___9. believe

___10. best

Word Group 2

___11. both

___12. brother

___13. build

___14. busy

___15. buy

___16. carry

___17. caught

___18. children

___19. city

___20. could

CHECKLISTS OF LEARNED WORDS

Word Groups 3 and 4

Word Group 3

___21. country

___22. cousin

___23. dear

___24. didn't

___25. different

___26. does

___27. doesn't

___28. done

___29. door

___30. drink

Word Group 4

___31. drop

___32. easy

___33. enough

___34. every

___35. eye

___36. face

___37. first

___38. forty

___39. girl

___40. give

CHECKLISTS OF LEARNED WORDS

Word Groups 5 and 6

Word Group 5

___41. good

___42. great

___43. have

___44. head

___45. heard

___46. here

___47. house

___48. hurt

___49. idea

___50. it's

Word Group 6

___51. knew

___52. large

___53. light

___54. listen

___55. look

___56. mail

___57. make

___58. many

___59. measure

___60. more

CHECKLISTS OF LEARNED WORDS

Word Groups 7 and 8

Word Group 7

___61. often

___62. once

___63. only

___64. people

___65. perfect

___66. piece

___67. question

___68. said

___69. school

___70. since

Word Group 8

___71. sister

___72. sometimes

___73. sudden

___74. that's

___75. there

___76. they

___77. think

___78. this

___79. thought

___80. through

CHECKLISTS OF LEARNED WORDS

Word Groups 9 and 10

Word Group 9

___81. told

___82. tree

___83. trip

___84. truck

___85. two

___86. until

___87. use

___88. usually

___89. watch

___90. when

Word Group 10

___91. where

___92. which

___93. who

___94. whole

___95. winner

___96. won't

___97. wouldn't

___98. write

___99. year

___100. young

CONGRATULATIONS! 😊

You can feel good about your great effort, after learning all 100 vocabulary words!

Now, you are ready to go on to Level 2 in the Vocabulary Series of the *Joy of Knowing How to Learn*.

LIST OF STUDY WORDS

1. about	26. does	51. knew	76. they
2. again	27. doesn't	52. large	77. think
3. always	28. done	53. light	78. this
4. another	29. door	54. listen	79. thought
5. anyone	30. drink	55. look	80. through
6. asked	31. drop	56. mail	81. told
7. beautiful	32. easy	57. make	82. tree
8. before	33. enough	58. many	83. trip
9. believe	34. every	59. measure	84. truck
10. best	35. eye	60. more	85. two
11. both	36. face	61. often	86. until
12. brother	37. first	62. once	87. use
13. build	38. forty	63. only	88. usually
14. busy	39. girl	64. people	89. watch
15. buy	40. give	65. perfect	90. when
16. carry	41. good	66. piece	91. where
17. caught	42. great	67. question	92. which
18. children	43. have	68. said	93. who
19. city	44. head	69. school	94. whole
20. could	45. heard	70. since	95. winner
21. country	46. here	71. sister	96. won't
22. cousin	47. house	72. sometimes	97. wouldn't
23. dear	48. hurt	73. sudden	98. write
24. didn't	49. idea	74. that's	99. year
25. different	50. it's	75. there	100. young

Made in the USA
Middletown, DE
09 September 2019